Copyright 2012 by JoEllen Claypool
Published by Valley Walker Press
New Plymouth, ID 83655

Cover designed by Gina Burns
Edited by Cyndi Cook, Ruthilyn Sparks, and Jane Freund

For more information, please contact:
Valley Walker Press
P.O. Box 288
New Plymouth, ID 83655

valleywalkerpress@hotmail.com

First printing 2012

ISBN – 978-0-9857658-1-1
Library of Congress Control Number 2012942234

To order additional copies of this book, contact Valley Walker Press at the address listed above.

Dedication

I dedicate this book to my extended church family. I would not have been able to grow in my walk with God if I hadn't been exposed to so many different personalities and situations, each teaching me more about myself and the true love that God has for each one of us.

Acknowledgements

Thank you to my husband and children for being so patient with me during this process. My husband encouraged me daily to write and would pray over me every night that I would be granted success with this project. He was so patient when I would tell him that I was going to sit down and write for 30 minutes and then join the family again three hours later! My kids understood what I was doing and would show interest by asking questions about the process. I could not have done this without them cheering me on and believing in me.

I also have to take this opportunity to thank Jane Freund, author and publisher, who provided an opportunity for me to learn about the business side of writing. After including some of my work in An Eclectic Collage Volume II: Relationships of Life, she voiced her heart by saying, "I know there are people out there that know how to write, but then do not know what to do with it." She graciously allowed me to cling to her while she taught me how to get involved with book signings. She also helped me understand the marketing and distributing duties, ultimately giving me the courage to pursue my life's dream of becoming a published author. Thank you, Jane, for your encouragement and for keeping me grounded!

Thank you Cyndi, Ruthilynn, and Jane who took the time to edit my work and gave me such great feedback! I was told by another author and friend, Wynette, that our book projects are like our children. We become very attached to them and we need to take care who looks after our children. I know that Cyndi, Ruthilynn and Jane took care of my "child" as if it were their own. Thank you ladies for the gentle truth that you spoke to help me make the changes that were needed.

I thank my folks, my husband's folks, my brothers and their wives for being my biggest fans and expressing how proud they are of me. They helped me promote my first project, getting the word out about my new passion. God has surrounded me with encouragers who kept me from losing heart in the overwhelming times.

Thanks to you all!

CONTENTS

Foreword

When my friend, JoEllen, asked me to read her book, I was so excited for a multitude of reasons. I knew that JoEllen would be an amazing author. I knew that she had a passion for writing and had always wanted to pursue that dream. Mostly though, I knew the topic she was writing about and I knew it would be a blessing from God for anyone who was led to read it.

JoEllen has such an amazing love for God and trusts Him with her heart and soul. She shines with the light of the grace and peace that only God can provide for His truly faithful children. That is why He would bless her in her endeavors to help Christian women who share a faith in the Almighty Father.

As excited as I was to get started, I unfortunately let life get in the way....or did I? I didn't read the draft of JoEllen's book for awhile, but I know now that that too was a gift from God. He knew when I would need to read it; when I would need to read those words of truth, those words of encouragement, those words of conviction. I read them at the exact time that God intended in order to give me hope, strength, love, and peace.

We all have baggage in our lives. The depth of the wounds caused by that trauma is widely varied. But, if we trust our Lord to heal those wounds and to provide the strength, love, grace, and peace that we desperately need, He will provide it.

It really hit me in the head and the heart when JoEllen talks about making a choice in living in your –"I'm the victim mentality"- or making a choice to move through and past it and live for God, not for anyone or anything else. I do have a choice; I just have to make it. That doesn't mean things will always be smooth as silk, but we can choose to wallow or to be victorious. This is what God knew I would need to hear and when I would need to hear it. Isn't our God amazing!

The other amazing part about reading her book was hearing her stories and learning the lessons through her again about being a Christian woman of God, which can be difficult, whether you are a Pastor's wife or other Christian wife. Submitting your life to a man as the Lord instructs is not an easy thing to do; it takes a great deal of strength and faith in God. Unfortunately it isn't a one time decision and you're done. Oh no, it is a decision that has to be made on a daily and often hourly basis! This is what Jo reminded me of again in her book. I revisited and was reminded of the many blessings that she and her family have received because she is Christian woman who obeys her Heavenly Father.

JoEllen wanted to write a book to help pastors' wives understand the trials and the blessing of standing by their pastor husband and supporting them in their quest to lead their congregations to deeper faith in God. Pastors get training in theology either formally or informally, dependent on the will of God. However, there is no class entitled Being a Pastor's Wife 101, or even Godly Wife 200. What a shame!

When my own husband was called to be a pastor in the rural church where he had been filling the pulpit, I went through a plethora of extreme emotions in a matter of seconds. I was excited for the wonderful opportunity we would have to share the Word of God with others, but I was panicked- what if they didn't listen? I was proud of my husband for the hard work he had already demonstrated for this body of people, but what if they truly didn't accept him or his leadership in the path of faith? I felt blessed to be able to do my part to further the Kingdom of God, but what if I messed it up?

Can you can see where this is going? I wish there had been a book I could have scrambled to purchase and read so I would have known what to expect and how to move forward in the will of God. I wish I would have had JoEllen's book. It was truly a gift from God through her words. It spoke directly to my heart. I felt inspired, uplifted, and renewed. Her words gave me perspective, grounding, and guidance in regard to my role as the wife of a pastor.

As part of her book she asked questions of various pastors' wives. It was interesting to learn about their experiences, their successes, and their fears. I wasn't alone in my joy or fear. Even just re-reading the words I had answered to JoEllen's questions gave me perspective – that is the person I am in God, not the lump of emotional baggage that was sitting in the chair the Saturday morning I read it.

Wow! When I sat down to read my friend's manuscript, I had no idea it would have the tremendous impact it did. I encourage you, whether you are a pastor's wife or the wife of any Christian man, to read JoEllen's book. I have faith that God will give you the message you need to hear if you read with an open heart to Him.

Cyndi Cook

Heart Condition:
Wanting to help

1A
INTRODUCTION

This section was named Chapter 1A because many times people do not read the introduction of a book but skip right to the first chapter. (I know I cannot be the only one.) Before proceeding, I felt a few explanations were necessary.

The role of Pastor's Wife is the most difficult job I have ever had. I have worked in many different fields ranging from cleaning offices and being a cook to being a bank teller and medical transcriptionist. When comparing and seeing what all of my other jobs had in common, I realized it was the fact that I had a training period. The guidelines were laid out very clearly as to what was expected of me as an employee and what I could expect from them as my employer. The position of Pastor's Wife does not come with that luxury. Another pastor's wife summed it up well by saying, "You can't prepare for this. It is on the job training." Constant training; and just when you think you might have a few things figured out, you are faced with a new situation.

I am....ok I have *become* very thankful for the opportunity God has given me and truly regret wasting five years trying to make the ministry all about me instead of all about Him. There have been many ups and downs in my experience. I believe we can fall into spending much of our time trying to pretend that being in this role is wonderful and we are the perfect little family and nothing bad comes our way. If we admit that we struggle, that might come across to people that we do not have enough faith. Heaven forbid that we should admit that we have a bad day once in a while or that we struggle with certain issues.

I am a list follower. That is my comfort zone. I like to be able to check things off to see that I have accomplished a certain task or characteristic. When I first entered the role as a pastor's wife, I wanted so badly to be able to find a book that would give me a list telling me exactly what to do and when to do it. I never found that book so figured I would write one. My main purpose is to give women an idea of what to expect in this position; maybe not a list, but an idea of things that they may encounter and how to deal with them. I want to be real with you. I want you to know that other women can relate to what you are going through emotionally as you strive to figure out what your role is as a pastor's wife.

Let me make one thing clear; I do NOT have it all figured out. This is what I went through. This is what worked for me. I wanted to share with others what I was discovering so that maybe their transition could be a little easier. As I have talked to other wives in the ministry, they have shared their heart and their hurts that were so similar to mine. I knew that they truly understood me. That is what I want for you, the reader, to know; that you are not alone, that there are women who do understand.

This book tells about the transformation in my heart, as a woman who considered herself to be a good Christian, who had grown up in the church, who found herself in the position where she had to decide what life was truly about. You will notice hearts at the beginning of each chapter. These tell what my heart condition was during that time period. There were times that my heart was not very healthy, but I encourage you to hang around to the end because it truly does come full circle. I will share many personal experiences with you to show you God's power and what He does through those situations.

Heart Condition:
Confusion

1B
WHERE DO I BELONG?

Have you ever thought, "What is my purpose? Why am I here?" I have entertained those thoughts, but answers would not appear. Instead Defeat would tower over me and raise its gruff voice telling me I had nothing to offer, no special talents, no particular gifts. I was a waste of space. Defeat would lead me to the trap of comparing myself to others and to their creative abilities and whisper, "See what they have? You could never do that. You look like a fool when you even try." I would hide so that nobody else would see how worthless I was. If I sat quietly and did not draw attention to myself, nobody would know I was there. I could escape another day of humiliation.

What a horrible place to be in life! One thing I have learned as I have gotten to know people is that I am not the only one who struggles with this. People deal with it in different ways, however. Some of us hide while others overcompensate by acting extremely confident. Do you sometimes feel that you're the only one who has hard times? "I am so hard done by. I am the ONLY one who struggles with this issue. NOBODY else could possibly understand." It's a trap; the self-pity-I'm-a-victim-nobody-else-matters-it's- all-about-me trap. And it's a deep one that is difficult to climb out of once you have fallen into it. Even if you can muster up the strength and courage to find a foothold to start climbing, Defeat is right there to make the dirt crumble under your feet, making you slide back down, sometimes deeper than before.

This is a constant spiritual battle that I have to fight. My best friend told me one time that I needed to quit playing the victim and trying to make every situation about me. I know that sounds harsh, but it was very true. In my defense, I explained that since I *have* been a victim in my life, the cycle is hard to break. That conversation, however, did bring me to a new awareness. Now I try to evaluate the situation before I react by asking, #1 "am I trying to be the victim" and #2 "am I trying to make it about me"?

This battle is always hanging on my shoulders trying to weigh me down. I have to continually remind myself that I am fearfully and wonderfully made (**Psalm 139:14**). In one of my slumps, I had read **Isaiah 53:3** - referring to Jesus Christ, "He was despised and rejected by others, a man of suffering and familiar with pain." Reading this made me feel....well pathetic, actually, because even though some of the things I have gone through in my life have been bad and have been real, I cannot consider myself to be a person familiar with suffering and pain. I do not have to go very far to see that I really have it pretty good.

God knew this concept was starting to sink in and reaffirmed it that same week for me. My son, Eli, had been hurt as he had scraped his belly on a branch of the tree he had been climbing. One of the men from the church noticed that Eli was getting ready to cry and said, "Bet it's nothing compared to what Jesus went through."

I had never heard anybody respond to a child's injury quite like that before and now it seems strange. I knew God had put me within earshot and had those words come off his tongue to remind me to be thankful that I am not *familiar* with pain.

Fighting these battles of listening to the voice of Defeat and trying to avoid the trap distracted me even more when trying to figure out what my purpose was. Calming the noise in my mind enough to sort it out was hard.

So what was the answer? I knew the coined answer; I needed to pray and go to the Word. I absolutely needed to do this, but with my mind so full of chaos, I knew I would not be able to be quiet enough to hear God. One thing I added to that was planting reminders of God's promises all around the house on note papers and writing verses in bright pink or dark red lipstick on my bathroom mirror. I did not wear lipstick so figured this was a good use for the ones I had laying around. This forced me to face the truths of God's Word first thing in the morning, throughout the day, and before I went to bed at night.

Also, verse memorization is a good tool to use at times such as these. At first, I had a million reasons why I could not memorize. However when I really stopped and thought about all of the names, numbers, addresses, etc. that I memorize every day, I found that I really had no excuse. I just needed to make a habit of looking at my daily verses, the same as I made it a habit to brush my teeth. As the words of these verses began to penetrate my heart and started calming my spirit, *then* I was able to hear God's voice clearer. As soon as I was able to instill in my mind that life really had nothing to do with me, my journey became easier.

| **Occurrence:** |
| Defeat |
| |
| **Solution:** |
| Reminders |

I could write another book filled with my favorite verses and promises of God, but these are a sample of the verses I used. I'm sure there are many that have touched your life personally.

Psalm 139:14 - I praise You because I am fearfully and wonderfully made; Your works are wonderful, I know that full well.

I John 3:1 - See what great love the Father has lavished on us, that we should be called children of God! And that is what we are!

I Peter 5:7 - Cast all your cares on Him because He cares for you.

Romans 8:1 - There is therefore now no condemnation for those who are in Christ Jesus.

Deuteronomy 31:6 - Be strong and courageous. Do not be afraid or terrified because of them, for the Lord your God goes with you; He will never leave you nor forsake you.

Philippians 4:13 - I can do all things through Christ who strengthens me.

Hebrews 4:16 - Let us therefore come boldly unto the throne of grace, that we may obtain mercy and find grace to help in times of need.

Proverbs 3:26 - For the Lord shall be thy confidence, and shall keep thy foot from being taken.

Genesis 21: 22b - God is with you in everything you do.

I Samuel 2:9 - He will guard the feet of his faithful servants

Heart Condition:
Fulfilling a need

2
A PRAYER ANSWERED

Wondering where my specific place was in the world seemed to constantly nag at the back of my mind. I did not just sit around waiting for an answer to come though. I tried different things. I was searching.

To give you a little background: in 1999, my husband, our three sons and I had moved from our hometown of Gillette, Wyoming (population around 20,000) to New Plymouth, a much smaller town (population 1500) in Idaho. We had transferred with my husband's job as a manufactured home salesman (I was trained to not call them trailer houses).

The first day I ventured out on my own in New Plymouth, I witnessed small town hospitality at its finest. I had just registered the two older boys for school. With my one year old son, Christopher, in tow, I stopped at the only restaurant in town to grab a bite for breakfast. We were the only two there. After taking my order and delivering my meal, the waitress and cook both joined me at the table and visited with me like we were long lost sisters. With the hook that they had a great youth group, the waitress invited our family to the First Baptist Church, one of the bigger churches in town. That was very appealing since our sons, JJ and David were 9 and 13 , respectively.

We attended the First Baptist the following weekend and were welcomed by all we met. A schedule of classes and events was handed to us and we were encouraged to check them out. I decided to attend one of the women's Bible studies held in a home just a block away from where we lived which enabled me meet some of the other women of the church.

I got very involved in the church after that. I helped with Sunday school and eventually moved into teaching Sunday school, children's church and an after school youth group.

One other thing that you may need to understand about me is that doing these things was completely out of my comfort zone. I have been an introvert all of my life. Even up until the day we moved, I would have rather crossed the street than have to take the chance on looking up and saying hi to somebody. People scared me to death; another result of allowing Defeat into my life.

When we left our hometown, I had made up my mind to be different. Nobody in our new town knew how shy I was. I could be whoever I wanted to be and they would never know the difference. So I dug right in and tried to make friends. It was good, but I still did not feel that even all of this involvement was "it".

With a little coaxing, my husband, Dallas, was also becoming very involved. At first, doing so was hard for him. He worked about ten miles away, which was not far, but it prevented him from getting to know the people in our own community. On the other hand, I worked at the only bank in town, which helped me get to know most of the people in New Plymouth before Dallas did. I would encourage him the best I could and he did start getting acquainted with the men of the church. He began attending various groups eventually leading some of them and then was asked to become a deacon.

A series of events started to unfold (I hadn't realized yet that events leading up to this had been put into action a long time ago). One evening in 2006, a call came for my husband. A friend of ours explained that a little Southern Baptist country church he attended was in need of a pastor. This man had heard Dallas speak a couple of times and was very enthusiastic in his urging him to fill the position.

Incidentally, we had been attending a church leadership class at First Baptist using the Bible Training Center for Pastors. That very night we just *happened* to be talking about the duties of a pastor. Coincidence? I think not. We were told there would be a business meeting that week and that we should attend because the association was planning on closing the doors to the church.

Wednesday night came, the night of the meeting. Dallas and I decided it couldn't hurt to go and at least see what was happening. We drove 20 minutes until we spotted a sign that said "The Middle of Nowhere" or was it "Exit 17"? Anyway , they were synonymous. We came to a stop sign and spotted a café/gas station/convenient store across the street and a campground south from that. We turned right and about half a mile up the road on the right hand side stood a big tan building with white trim, the color being the only thing that distinguished it from a barn. The worn sign in front announcing Sunday school and Worship hours assured us that we had reached our destination. The minute we opened the front door of the church, I knew. THIS is where I belonged. I had never felt a feeling so strong or so sure and with no doubt attached.

As we entered the small foyer, we stood between two small rooms. The one on the right appeared to be the pastor's office and the one on the left, a library. A few feet forward, the foyer opened into one large multipurpose room. Looking to the left I spotted a door along the wall leading into a classroom. At the front of the room was an organ. There was also a stage, raised only about one foot off the ground. Gazing at the far wall in front of me I could see a door leading into a kitchen area and another small classroom to the right of that. The walls were overwhelmingly large and empty extending down from the 24 foot ceiling. The space in between was filled with fifteen dark stained, wooden pews. They had long red cushions, which clashed a bit with the multi-colored carpet showing predominantly purple specks and a solid purple strip in front of the stage. The stage was covered with the same speckled carpet.

We turned our attention to the eight people seated at a long table on the north end of the big room. There were two tiny older ladies, sisters we would later find out, with shoulder length gray hair, unkempt polyester pants and plaid long sleeve shirts.

There was a big old bear of a man. Suspenders over a white t-shirt held up his baggy blue jeans. He had a long, white beard and mustache and eyes that twinkled like Santa himself. He was there with his wife who sat, nervously running her fingers through her short hair. Although she was laughing and trying to be a part of the conversation with the others, I could tell she on the verge of tears. Another couple sat together, an extremely thin man in a blue, short sleeved mechanics shirt, trying to look relaxed and confident as he laid back lazily in one of the tan lawn chairs they were all sitting in. The woman sitting next to him had very short, brown hair. She was wearing fuzzy blue slippers on her feet but dressed as though she had just come from working an office job. Her contagious laugh filled the room and when she spoke there was a hint of a southern accent.

One other white haired gentleman was there. He was a big man with glasses and a short sleeved plaid shirt and a big ceramic mug of coffee in his hand.

Lastly we spotted the familiar face of a middle aged woman, thin with short, gray hair. She had a smile that lit up the entire room and a tone in her voice that made you feel that you were the only one in her world. We had met her at the First Baptist Church years before. She greeted us with a warm welcome, hugging us both and telling us how happy she was to see us. She offered us a seat and a cup of coffee, which we eagerly accepted after coming in out of the chill of the February air.

The atmosphere seemed very tense as a tall, medium build, silver haired gentleman came in and introduced himself. He was the one sent to help the people understand the situation. I listened to him explain casually, in his obvious southern accent, why he was suggesting that they close their doors. I watched the reactions of each of the members. Voices started to rise when questions were being interjected and it quickly became clear that they did not understand a lot of the church politics. They just wanted a place to worship.

I did not know these people at all, but my heart felt like it was breaking in two. I wept with them as they tried to defend themselves and recounted stories on the different stages the church had gone through. I could visualize the little white church they spoke of that used to sit in what was now the parking lot. I could smell the smoke from the wood stove that they said had to be used to heat the church. I could feel the excitement that they must have had as they worked in unity, laying the foundation and erecting the walls of this new building. It must have seemed massive compared to the tiny room they had been worshiping in for so long. What an accomplishment that must have been! Now they were being told it was all for naught. I wept.

I watched to see what my husband would do to "fix" this situation. (He is a fixer, you know). I did not know what reaction to expect from him. His body language gave no hint as he sat forward with his elbows on his knees, styrofoam coffee cup in his hands and his eyes fixated on the floor. He finally spoke up when the gentleman opened it up for more discussion. Dallas introduced himself and offered to be a guest speaker until they were able to find a pastor. The facilitator's reaction came quickly, "What church are you from?"

My husband sighed, because he knew what was coming. "I am from the First Baptist Church."

"Oh, so you're an American Baptist," the man said, almost with disgust. I felt he was resisting the urge to roll his eyes. I had a teenage boy in the house and knew the tone that went with that body language and he was using "the tone".

"Yes, I am, but I did not know that until this morning when my pastor told me you would try to use that against me. I just want to love God's people," Dallas' deep voice kept an even tone.

The gentleman packed up his things and abruptly told the church members to do what they wanted, but they had better use caution. (I do want to mention here that we did build a relationship with this man and, although I am sure we frustrated him, he did become a friend).

The people approached us afterwards and expressed their appreciation for us being there. My husband jotted down our phone number for them and again reiterated that he would be willing to be a speaker for them as they tried to find another pastor. They were eager to have us out that next Sunday. We were happy to oblige and Dallas gave a great inspirational sermon, urging them to Keep On Keepin' On. Two weeks later they hired him.

They hired him.

That was a hard thing to wrap our minds around. Now what? Dallas had no formal training as a pastor. He had taught adult Sunday school and some teenage groups and was taking the church leadership classes. He had filled in at the pulpit a time or two, having six months to plan out his sermon but certainly nothing on a weekly basis. This bothered me at first and I was always asking God, "Why are You using us? We are not trained to do this." It helped me understand more at one point when I read that God does not always call the qualified but qualifies those He calls.

It all started to make sense. NOW, we were able to look back and see when the events leading up to this began to unfold. We had often talked about why we moved. It made no sense at the time. We lived in the same town as all of our family. Neither of us had ever been away from our parents for any great length of time. I had a good job as a medical transcriptionist in the pathology department of the hospital. When Dallas' boss asked if I would be on board with his job transfer, I asked him if he was going to make it worth it and pointed out the things I was giving up to do this. He assured me it would be. Six months after the move, that job ended and there we were.

However, we know now that this move HAD to take place for us to be where we are today. God had given us a peace about moving and had drawn us to this little town. Out of all of the towns in this area we could have considered, He made this one stick out to us because this was where we were going to be able to get involved. The town was small enough that people would get to know us on a personal level. This was where the people were that God would use to see Dallas' potential, to mentor him and to use the tactic of iron sharpening iron to encourage him to seek out Scripture. To see how God orchestrated this whole seven year time period was overwhelming to us. He knew how to get us to the right place at the right time so that we could be used as Kingdom builders.

> **Occurrence:**
> Unexpected surprises
>
> **Solution:**
> Be ready!

I AM A PASTOR'S WIFE

I am a pastor's wife?

Shouldn't I have a bun in my hair
to wear that title?
Shouldn't I have a modest dress
for each day of the week?

I think I'm supposed to speak softly
and be gentle to all.
I think I'm supposed to play piano
and sing like an angel.

Don't I have to bake
and have grand pot lucks?
Don't I have to have
weekly tea parties for the ladies?

Well, I wear my hair down.
I only have pants.
I can be rather loud,
not gentle at all
I can plunk a few keys
but can't carry a tune
I hate to bake
And I don't drink tea.

I am a pastor's wife.

JoEllen Claypool
10/01/11

Heart Condition:
Searching

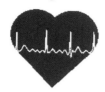

3
WHAT IS A PASTOR'S WIFE?

So my journey as a pastor's wife began.

I was filled with images of what a pastor's wife should look like. I pictured the physical appearance as being a quiet woman with a flowery, modest dress, her hair in a neat bun and always right beside her husband. Inwardly, I pictured a gentle woman who was soft spoken, never raising her voice.

Years had passed since I had experienced any personal interaction with a pastor's wife. I had one acquaintance who would later become a good resource for me, but in the beginning I did not have much to go on. However, I did have the desire to be a *good* pastor's wife.

I found great difficulty connecting with anybody who could offer me any advice. Introducing myself to people was never my strong suit and I was not sure what my options were as far as meeting other women in the ministry. Functions that I did see that were happening were usually held in the Utah area or in the cities, but for the women in the more rural areas, there did not seem to be many opportunities to meet. I did go to a few events with Dallas and was very intimidated by some of the women, this coming more from my own personality than theirs.

A definite difference existed between the wives of the country preachers and the wives of the city preachers. The women from the smaller areas were more reserved while those from the city, appeared very confident and wore beautiful clothes and jewelry and exhibited very outgoing personalities. I thought I would be able to fake it and fit right in since I was "one of them" now, but they each had a very strong presence. When I would gather the courage to try to interact, my old pal, Defeat, would show up, exchanging his gruff voice for sweeter ones, but with the same message as before. I would cling to my husband as we tried to make casual conversation with the others until the function would be over.

I am reminded of a scene in the movie, "Michael", in which John Travolta portrays the famous archangel. When the news reporters arrive to interview him, he is seen sauntering down the stairs, shabbily dressed and a cigarette hanging out of his mouth. He sits down at the table for breakfast and sloppily eats his cereal with entirely too much sugar, although he announces later you cannot have too much sugar with which I concur. One of the reporters (a supposed angel expert) attempts to describe what she thought an angel would look like. Her first words were "I thought angels would be cleaner and ....". The angel helps her out by stating, "Halos. Inner light." She nods as if those were the words she was looking for to which Michael leans toward her and responds, "I'm not that kind of angel."

That has become my motto. "I'm not that kind of pastor's wife." I needed only a couple of meetings to figure out that I did not really fit in to this pastors' wives group. One thing I did learn right away was that my husband and I were the only ones in this valley of Southern Baptist preachers...without a southern accent.

My focus at that point was to start becoming comfortable in whom God made me to be. I had to stop comparing myself to others and figure out what kind of pastor's wife *God* wanted me to be.

I guess I just assumed that now that we were in the ministry that we would automatically be accepted by others in the ministry and respected as equals. The reality was that there were a lot of people that did not feel we belonged in this position. My husband had to do a lot of proving before some would even look his way. Dallas did not let that distract him though. He was just what this tiny congregation needed and, I believe, was the one God had chosen to grow this particular church body. The doors had almost been closed on a church that was still alive; like pronouncing a patient dead before even checking the pulse.

Just as it took time for this circle of people to accept us, it also took time for family and friends to accept what we were doing and I was not quite prepared for that. Everybody has their story and Dallas and I definitely had a before Christ and after Christ testimony. We knew what we had been saved from. We knew how close we came to going to hell so we truly did love God with ALL our heart, soul, mind and strength. However, many people define you *by* your past and do not let you escape it.

I suppose I expected everybody to be excited to hear about how the church was growing. Quite the opposite was true. Everytime I tried to bring up the subject of church, people would not respond to my statements. Instead they would get up and walk out of the room with no explanation. It was the most awkward thing I had ever experienced.

I could not understand what people were thinking. I finally got the courage to ask a friend (one that I trusted to tell me the truth) about what was being said. When I got to their house and seated myself, I slapped my hand in the middle of the kitchen table and said, "Okay, lay it on me. What the heck is going on? People do not want to get within ten feet of me when I start talking about church."

"You want to know what's happening? We're all laughing at you! We know what kind of past Dallas has," his jolliness made the statement seem even more mocking.

"Don't you believe that God can change someone's life?" I asked, feeling like I had just been punched in the gut but not wanting to show it.

"Not that drastically," he laughed.

"Okay. I just needed to know where I stand and now I do. It won't be brought up again."

I let that all sink in as I headed back home and it just made me sad. I could not really blame them. Family and friends are the ones who have witnessed us at our absolute worst in regards to behavior. It probably did seem very hypocritical to them.

My next step was to determine how I was going to deal with this situation. I decided it would be best to brush it off and not dwell on what others were thinking of us. I believed with all my heart that this was God's decision and not ours. In fact at this point, I couldn't figure out who would CHOOSE to be in this profession. I needed to push forward.

My focus came back to what certain image I felt expected to portray. I was not so worried about the outward appearance at this point, but more of the tasks I was to be in charge of.

I remember one of the gentlemen at the church approaching me one Sunday and asking, "Is it the role of the pastor's wife to…" . I interrupted him and said, "The role of the pastor's wife is whatever you say the role of the pastor's wife is." So that is how I maneuvered for awhile until it came to a point I knew boundaries had to be set. People quickly took advantage of my attitude that I was just there to do what I was told by whoever told me to do it. The truth that had to register with me and with others was the fact that I was Dallas' helpmeet and when certain requests from others interfered with that, a boundary line had to be drawn.

I decided to get a hold of the acquaintance I had mentioned earlier. Her name is Diane and she was happy to meet me for coffee. Listening to her story was comforting because it was very similar to ours. She was more than eager to offer me advice because she also did not have a clue what to do when she first started and knew, firsthand, how I was craving someone to show me the ropes. She said one thing that day that I will never forget. She told me my main job was to **protect my husband.**

Occurrence:
Rejection
Solution:
Be confident in whom God has created you to be

Occurrence:
Being taken advantage of
Solution:
Set boundaries

4
TO SERVE AND PROTECT-
PART I

Protect my husband? What did that mean? What did that look like? I always thought the man's role was to protect the woman. As we carried on in the ministry, I pondered that advice. I did know I was to be my husband's helpmeet and to submit and I was more than happy to do so.

Be prepared to defend what the Bible says about this as women get tired of hearing about it. It is important, though, that the women you may counsel acknowledge their husbands as the spiritual leader of the home. (**James 3:17-18** - But the wisdom that comes from heaven is first of all purer, then peace-loving, considerate, submissive, full of mercy and good fruit impartial and sincere. Peacemakers who sow in peace reap a harvest of righteousness; **I Peter 3:1** - Wives in the same way, submit yourselves to your own husbands; **Colossians 3:18** - Wives submit yourselves to your husbands as is fitting to the Lord; **Ephesians 5:21** - Submit to one another **out of reverence for Christ).** We cannot just pick and choose which parts of the Bible we want to follow and which parts we do not.

Through discussion, some women have voiced that to submit makes them feel that they have no control. Others have said they feel it would make them look weak. I believe that quite the opposite is true. A very strong woman is needed to control her tongue and use it for good (**Proverbs 15:4** - The soothing tongue is a tree of life but a perverse tongue crushes the spirit; **Proverbs 12:18** - The words of the reckless pierce like swords but the tongue of the wise brings healing).

Supporting her husband and building him up takes a strong woman, even if she doesn't agree with everything he is doing. It takes a strong woman to give a gentle answer **(Proverbs 15:1** - A gentle answer turns away wrath, but a harsh word stirs up anger; **I Peter 3:4** - [Your beauty] ….should be that of your inner self, the unfading beauty of a gentle and quiet spirit which is of great worth in God's sight).

Choosing words carefully takes strength so as not to come across as a nag or make her husband feel that she is putting him down. **(Proverbs 27:15** - A quarrelsome wife is like a constant dripping on a rainy day). I do understand that this concept can be abused by some men, but when done right, it is a very beautiful image of marriage. (**Proverbs 31:25** - She is clothed with strength and dignity)

I was aware that being a helpmeet was important, but I felt that there had to be more to it than just supporting him. I do not mean to minimize that at all. At times, we may forget that we should be a support to our husband in all areas. Fear may be holding us back from supporting him in his job because what he is doing may be out of our comfort zone. I see this a lot in the ministry; the husband gets "called" to be more involved and that may not have been the direction the wife thought their marriage would ever go. Certain positions our husbands take on may overwhelm us as women when we try to balance family life with their new job. Wives may not want all of the responsibility that may be expected of her in this transition. Believe me, I understand. There were times I could comprehend how a wife could mentally "check out". There were times I thought, "I wonder if the women were on board with the change at first and then as expectations piled up, it just got to be too much." I had a pastor and his wife tell me at the beginning of our ministry that there were several occasions where they packed a suitcase and drove to the edge of town and contemplated whether they should just pick a direction and keep on driving.

For those who have children at home, I believe the husband and children are that woman's first mission field and definite boundaries can be set and worked out between her and her husband so that nothing interferes with that. Communication is the key.

Many women work today, however and there is nothing wrong with that. It has caused a struggle for some, though, knowing that they have worked really hard for a career and are unsure of how to encourage their husband if he has been called to the ministry. They feel that they have to make a choice between helping them in the ministry or working. Communication. Is your husband expecting you to quit your job? You can certainly work AND encourage him. Talk with him.

There are times I have to come straight out and ask my husband "What do you need from me right now? What are your expectations?" Here are some ways we can encourage and protect our husbands.

PROTECT HIS EGO

As far as supporting our husbands, much of this advice is not only for pastors' wives but also for all Christian wives. I feel we need to be our husbands' biggest fan. Protect his ego. What does THAT look like?

What would you do if your favorite star walked through the front door? You would immediately drop what you were doing. You would cater to them and make sure they were comfortable. You would let them know how excited you were to see them.

I once heard someone say that the dog is usually more eager to see the husband walk through the door than the wife is. That really made me evaluate how I act when Dallas walks in the front door. It was true, I had to practically race the dog to the door. In fact, I started learning the signs. When our cocker spaniel started nervously pacing back and forth, sniffing at the front door and whimpering, I knew to get on my mark because my husband would be about a mile down the road and coming up the driveway any minute.

One habit I started getting into was choosing things that I could tell my husband that I admired about him or build him up in some aspect. My husband is a great father. He knows how to really talk to our kids and get them to open up about anything. He is a great speaker. His passions for God, for history and politics amaze me. Focus on the good things and build your husband up. There was a reason you fell in love and married him. Reflect on those things periodically.

Our husbands know their faults and do not need to be nagged about their shortcomings. As women, we can be rather critical. Fight through that. I was about to point out some things to Dallas one night and stopped and asked myself, "Do I really want to open that door; do I want to hear all of the shortcomings he sees in me?" That made me quickly change my mind.

PROTECT HIS SANITY

When you talk to your husband, use discernment. I tell my husband everything, but I wait for the "right time". **(Proverbs**

31:26 - She speaks with wisdom and faithful instruction is on her tongue). I try not to bombard Dallas when he first comes home, for instance, and instead of going to him with every little dilemma, I try to work things out for myself. If we can be big girls and figure things out on our own or chat with a girlfriend or family member (again, use discernment), sometimes that is best. Remember our husbands are dealing with their own issues plus the issues of everyone in the church. It will be helpful to your husband not to have one more thing he has to figure out. It is the same as household fixing. There may be small projects around the house that we can help with and take off of his plate.

I will admit right now, the first time I was told to find a friend that I could boo hoo to because that was too much to expect of my husband, I was not a happy camper. In fact I think I stopped reading the book after that sentence and figured it must have been a man who wrote it. It was. I did not think there was anything wrong with wanting my husband to be my only friend. I still don't, but I do understand his point. I want to be a help to my husband not a hindrance, weighing him down.

PROTECT HIS REPUTATION

Proverbs 31:10-12 - A wife of noble character who can find? She is worth far more than rubies. Her husband has full confidence in her and lacks nothing of value. She brings him good not harm all the days of her life.

Proverbs 31:23 - Her husband is respected at the city gate, where he takes his seat among the elders of the land.

Do not just build your husband up to *him* but also when you are around others. This can be hard for us because we, as women, like to gossip in the name of "venting". Even if the things are true, we need to protect our husbands' reputations. When you are in a group of people, make sure he is within earshot at times when you are sharing good things about him. Let your husband see that you adore him. If you hear negative things said about him, stand up and set the record straight.

PROTECT HIS INTERESTS

Truly listen when your husband is talking.   Housework will always be there. It is not going anywhere so take the time when he is in the talking mood and listen. It doesn't matter if it is something you are interested in or not (**Philippians 2:3-4** - Do nothing out of selfish ambition or vain conceit. Rather in humility, value others above yourselves, not looking to your own interests but each of you to the interests of others).

My husband loves to talk about politics, something that I have never understood. Jealousy would set in when friends of mine were able to have lengthy conversations about politics with Dallas. I did not like that one bit. So, I had a choice. I could be angry that my friends had more in common with my husband than I did or I could change. I started learning about politics. I began watching the news channel with him. I would watch the presidential debates and decide for myself who I wanted to vote for and why, instead of depending on him to learn about their views and tell me who to vote for. If I did not understand something, I would simply ask and he was always more than willing to explain it to me. The explanation was usually an hour long conversation, but that was that much more time I could show my husband I was interested in him.

PROTECT HIS SPACE

Let your husband have a little space to himself. Dallas has his "man cave" and when he is in his man cave, I leave him alone. I understand it can be frustrating if it appears that we are bustling around the house cooking and cleaning and taking care of the kids while our husbands are sitting out in the living room studying the Bible.

Wherever they decide to study, what we need to understand is that we are the ones that will benefit from that. When I see Dallas studying the Word outside of his man cave, I try to make things quiet for him. I take the kids outside or quiet them down so he can concentrate more.

When we allow our husbands time to study, they will be blessed and we will be blessed as they will teach us what they have learned that day. I don't know about you, but I need all the instruction I can get. Protect his relationship with God.

PROTECT HIS HEART

Another way to support and encourage your husband is by believing that what he is doing is right. If your husband is in the ministry, or any other profession for that matter, believe in his calling to do that. Study the attributes he has that make him good at his job and voice your admiration of those qualities.

Life is surrounding your husband, trying to tear him down in his thoughts about himself and about his ability to provide. Be ready to build him up during those times. Be perceptive and put yourself in his shoes. Think of the weight that is on his shoulders as a provider of the home. Protect his heart.

PROTECT HIS TIME

Protect your husband's time. One night Dallas and I were expecting a couple to come by. They were getting married the next evening. I received a phone call from the mother of the bride who was in a panic and asked, "Will you please tell these kids that they need to have a rehearsal tonight?" So I called them. They informed me they would not be there for their meeting that evening.

"I understand. However, tomorrow is your wedding and you really need to be here tonight to let us know how you want everything to go," I explained.

"Oh, I thought Pastor Dallas would just show up and do his pastor thing," came the voice of the young groom.

When I explained that this was their wedding, not ours and that is not how it works he said, "Oh, okay, well, we will be over in 15 minutes then."

As calmly as I could I replied, "No, you will need to wait until 8:00. I have not fed my family dinner yet so you will have to wait for us now."

I went to the house and explained the whole situation to Dallas. He looked at me and said "You did all that?"

I smiled and said "I guess that is what Diane meant when she said I had to protect you." I had protected his time. I realized then that my husband had a lot on his plate with preparing sermons, calling on people, teaching midweek studies, figuring out how to make the church grow and handling disputes when they came up. If there were things like this that came up, I could handle them without getting him involved and forcing him to have to make one more decision. It made me feel good. It empowered me and made me realize how important my role could be.

PROTECT HIS MIND

I became very watchful after that, watching for opportunities to help. From the beginning we did not have many people to really draw from to teach Sunday school and Children's Church except for one other woman, Coralee. She and I would team up to teach these classes. She also led the Wednesday night youth group which was much larger than Sunday's attendance. Since Dallas taught an adult study group that night, I helped Coralee with that as a way of protecting his mind from having to figure out who would take care of the kids.

There was a time I had to forego attending another class he taught because people in the class had children and could not come because they did not have a babysitter. My husband asked if I would help with that. That was where he needed me. It also allowed me to spend time getting to know and love these children and to know how to pray for each one.

Was it always easy? No. There were times I got bitter. I did not get to hear my husband preach and teach as much as I would have liked. I felt that I was really missing out. I would also get jealous that Dallas was able to build relationships with these people at a different level than I was able to; especially in the small groups. Those groups developed a trust with each other that I never got to experience because I was not in the class. It was not always easy.

PROTECT HIS HEALTH

Proverbs 31:14 - She is like the merchant ships. She brings her food from afar.

The first thing I think of whenever I see this verse is ... couponing! I know it has nothing to do with that, but I feel it is our responsibility as wives to be wise with the money that is being brought into the home and shop to get the most bang for the buck, as they say.

If that means going "afar", we should be willing to do that.

The Internet is full of many great couponing ideas and programs. There should be free coupon classes in your area. I have heard it said that it takes up a lot of your time. It does not have to. A couple of the biggest things you need to know is: only use coupons for things that you normally buy and don't use the coupon until that item goes on sale somewhere. Stay watchful.

Watch for the buy one get one free sales, especially on meat. You can really get some good deals with little time and effort. You don't have to go to ten different stores each week, but there may be times it will be worth your while to actually hit two or three.

If there are certain eating habits you feel are not healthy for your husband and family, the task falls on you to do what you can to change that. For example, if sweets are an issue, cut back or don't buy them. The task also falls on us to be an example in this area, which can be tough. If our families see us eating right and stocking our shelves with good healthy snacks, they will be less apt to crave the unhealthy snacks. Habits can be hard to break and it will take time.

The best advice my mom gave me on dinner menus was that our dinner plates should have lots of color. You should not serve potatoes or corn with fish. There is no color. Serve green beans instead. You get the idea.

You may hear that it costs too much to eat healthy. It can, but again it doesn't have to. I had never been big on gardening in the past, but when we moved out to the church, I was blessed with lots of land to put a garden. Slowly, I learned and experimented with different vegetables. I learned how to do some canning and how to grow and freeze potatoes.

Summertime brings the farmer's markets and the fruit stands which sell things at a very reasonable price. There really is nothing more satisfying than having a dinner that is prepared with things that you had a part in growing. We had a meal one evening with the fish my husband and sons had caught, homemade salsa, fresh radishes and lettuce with cucumbers and carrots.. It was beautiful, and colorful. I could not help but admire it and think, "We did this!"

Our husbands may not always think of putting their health first and may not suggest to you that they would like to start taking vitamins. One thing I have learned is that if I hand my husband vitamins while I am taking mine, he never tells me no. I've also noticed that if I serve a healthy chef salad instead of pizza, he never complains which tells me, we, as wives, have a lot of control in our husbands' health. Protect it.

PROTECT HIS MARRIAGE

Dallas and I agreed from the very beginning that the men would counsel the men and the women would counsel the women. Whenever there was an issue, I would visit with the woman. If we needed to get Dallas involved, he and I would both visit with her. In this position, I felt a strong need to protect my marriage. Emotional affairs can be easy to fall into and can be just as devastating as physical affairs.

If you think about it, people tend to "fall in love" with people who help them. With doctors it is very easy to think "I love you. You made the pain go away. You must really love me if you were willing to do that for me." It sounds silly but it happens. I have learned it is the same with pastors. They are feeding people God's Word. They are taking time with people, discipling and working one on one with them at times. Pastors help make sure individuals are understanding where comfort from life's troubles can be found. They are great listeners. We have seen some very prominent members of the ministry, local and national, that would fall into these traps and their marriages would fail. It scared me to death. I did not want to give the devil a foothold with my marriage and I was bound and determined to protect it in any way that I could.

Dallas and I both have the love language of touch so we hug everybody. We want them to know that we love them and that we are glad to see them. Sometimes that can be misconstrued and become an obstacle. We had to learn who we could do that with and who we could not.

There were times I had to bring it to my husband's attention. He didn't always see what was happening until I would point out, "Honey, they are laughing just a *little* too loud at your jokes…..the ones that aren't that funny." Women can spot if another woman is being more flirty than is appropriate easier than a man.

It was heartbreaking to me because I take the family of God very literal and so when I would see that women were taking the love being extended in the wrong context or men were misconstruing my hugs, it was very hard. Dallas and I agreed that when we saw a woman seeking the attention of my husband, I would need to move in and try to give her the attention she was needing, without getting jealous. It did not always work out that way. My husband made sure everybody knew that he was very married, but I had to learn to be very secure with my marriage and believe in what we had together.

There were times our personal insecurities would get in the way, but we would always work it out. Remember, the key – communication. Talk out your worries and fears with your husband. Talk about how to resolve them.

Occurrence:	Occurrence:
Anxiety	Your husband's full plate
Solution:	Solution:
Communication	Protect him!

5
TO SERVE AND PROTECT – PART II

Proverbs 31:17-22 - She sets about her work vigorously; her arms are strong for her tasks. She sees that her trading is profitable and her lamp does not go out at night. In her hand she holds the distaff and grasps the spindle with her fingers. She opens her arms to the poor and extends her hands to the needy. When it snows, she has no fear for her household for all of them are clothed in scarlet. She makes coverings for her bed; she is clothed in fine linen and purple.

Proverbs 31:27-28 - She watches over the affairs of her household and does not eat the bread of idleness. Her children arise and call her blessed; her husband also and he praises her.

Proverbs 31:31 - Honor her for all that her hands have done and let her works bring her praise at the city gate.

What about serving? Women are busy. I know that. The saying "A woman's work is never done" had to come from somewhere. Remember what I said though. Our family is to be our first mission field. I know that many women work and I understand how that can be. I was a working mom for several years. I remember being so overwhelmed when I would come home, knowing that after working all day I would then have a whole evening of work ahead of me. I would have tunnel vision as I walked through the front door and go directly to the kitchen and eat. Yes, food is my drug of choice It soothed me. It made my troubles go away for a while….as long as I was eating.

It can be done though, One of my favorite resources is the Fly Lady technique at www.flylady.net. She has some great little tactics to make housework manageable by breaking things into 15 minute chunks of time. Utilize the wisdom from this site.

SERVE – WHAT'S FOR DINNER, HONEY?

Do you cringe when you hear those words? Do you get tired of *everyday* having to think of yet another thing to make for dinner? I think we all do at some point. When I worked, I normally got off between 5:00 and 6:00 PM, which meant that the first thing that was taken care of when I got home or when Dallas came in for the night was to make dinner.

Dallas was a meat and potato man, but I did learn some things I could get away with after years of studying my husband. You may hear me use that phrase a lot because I read once that we are to be students of our husbands and it made an impact on me. Anyway, if Dallas had worked a lot physically that day, I would always try to have a meat meal or casserole available. However, if it was a pretty lax day or we had sports events to go to, I could get by with serving tacos, hot dogs, or one of his favorites - elbow macaroni and stewed tomatoes. On days that were iffy, I would warn him early what was going to be for dinner so that he was not looking forward to roast beef and potatoes and then disappointed when dinner time came. Now, I know this may not fly with some husbands, but you are a student of your husband. Figure out what you can get by with and still please him.

Two words– crock pot. Of course, there are always the ideas

of making dinners ahead of time and freezing them. The menu planning method is great also. You make out a menu for two weeks and that is what you base your grocery list on. A friend and I tried this and hung the menu on our refrigerators. Our husbands seemed to appreciate having an idea of what to look forward to each night. Also my boys would not ask me five times a day what we were having for dinner because they knew they could go look at the list.

SERVE – IS THERE EVER A TIME THAT DISHES ARE *NOT* IN THE SINK

I try to make sure that the dishes are done every night before I go to bed; washed and put away. I am okay with letting them sit in the drainer, but I have overheard my husband making comments to the kids that he likes to see them put away. Sometimes he will go ahead and do it so I try my best to take the extra few minutes and do that.

Moms, if you have older children, please delegate. I know we like to have control and it took me a long time to give that up, but it will help your schedule. My biggest issue with it, after I became a stay at home mom, was that I felt I should have no excuse for not getting the housework done myself. The truth is, there are lots of other things we have to keep us busy. Work something out with the children. There are times my boys will do the dishes during the week and then I will give them a break on the weekends or I will do lunch dishes if they do supper dishes.

SERVE – LET'S PLAY PICK UP STICKS....OR TOYS...OR CLOTHES....OR BOOKS

The other thing I try to do is pick up the living room and dining area and straighten everything up each night. My reason is purely selfish - I do not want to get up in the morning and immediately face work. I try to make things pleasant to my eye when I walk out of the bedroom. This takes effort for me. Though my house is not messy, it does seem cluttered. When I walk into other houses, my first question is always "Where are your piles? Why doesn't anybody else have piles?" I have become a bit more relaxed in this area. I used to feel that our house had to look like kids did not live there. Reality was, kids did live there.

I don't mind if they bring toys out in the living room to play with because I would rather have the kids be out amongst us during the day than hidden in their rooms. My guidelines, however, require the toys to be put away at night. I reclaim my book shelves by taking all of the items that do not belong there and distributing them to whom they do belong. My biggest pet peeve - Do Not Use My Living Room as Your Trash Can!!! I don't wait until night time to get the kids to pick up their empty water bottles and soda cans or food wrappers.

When I first quit my job, I tried to always start picking up the house at about 3:00 PM. That way my husband could walk into a clean house. That was one thing that always bothered me when I worked, so I tried to make sure that he did not have to deal with that same stress immediately after getting home. I was a first time homeschooling mom and there were days that I did not meet that 3:00 PM self-set curfew. One day Dallas came home early and I immediately apologized saying, "I am so sorry that the house has been messy lately when you come home. I should be able to get it all done and will work harder at it." His response lifted a huge weight off my shoulders. He said, "Honey, I would much rather live in a pig sty and know that you are playing with our children and spending time with them rather than live in an immaculate house and know that our children are being neglected." Wow, I thought that was incredibly sexy. Yes, pastors' wives are allowed to say 'sexy'.

SERVE – MAKE THE BED

In the mornings, the first thing I do is make my bed. My husband has never complained about how the house looks, but I do know one thing that blesses him is a made bed. Again, study your husband and find out if there are certain tasks that make him happy. If he doesn't really voice anything in particular, then keep this in mind - your home should be a safe haven for your husband. It is his castle. It should be a place that he can come in and be able to relax. I want my husband to enjoy coming home.

I was at a doctor's office a while back, filling out one of their many personal information forms. I always feel a bit sheepish when I write down homemaker in the blank labeled Occupation. This day was different. As I wrote that word, I heard a Shakespearean voice sound off inside my head as it dawned on me that, "*I . . . .. am a homemaker, I . . . . am a maker of homes.*" It was the first time I was proud of that title.

SERVE – LAUNDRY

I fall very short in the area of laundry, but try to keep up on it. What is it with the sock basket? I dread even looking at it. I look forward to the day that my husband and boys all have the same size hooves. I am going to go and buy several packages of the same style of socks. That way I will just have to worry about dividing them up evenly and not have to deal with matching them up.

Ironing is also something that is not listed under my strong qualities as a wife. I hate to iron. Usually Dallas would iron his clothes, if he felt they needed it. When it came time for Sunday morning though, I would get so incredibly distracted by the wrinkles in his clothes. That was one of my critical moments and instead of picking him apart about it, I fought through it and fixed it. I iron now.

Occurrence:
Finding Balance

Solution:
Study your husband
Delegate
Fly Lady technique

6

THE MAT - PICK IT UP, PUT IT DOWN

My heart to serve and protect my husband was definitely genuine. In fact, when I would see Dallas start a load of laundry or do the dishes, it drove me crazy. I explained to him that it made me feel very inadequate as a wife and that there is no excuse for it not being done. In turn, he told me that he did it when he saw I was busy with so many other things and felt I could use an extra hand. It took me awhile to get used to it and not take offense when he would help. This is the beautiful part of submission I was talking about. He sees my heart in wanting to help him and he, in turn, wants to bless me.

Getting the balance of what to be to my husband was easy compared to this next section. I had a very hard time knowing what my role was *in* the church. I immediately took on the janitor position. Our first weekend at the church, Dallas and my boys joined me in spending a whole day cleaning. We wanted to bless the people there and have it sparkly clean for Sunday morning. I may have stepped over my boundaries by doing this right away. Some things got moved and it threw people for a loop. I learned later that churches have actually split over situations like this.

Two days later (after the eight hours of cleaning, mind you) a piece of ceiling fell to the floor, spreading insulation everywhere. Shingles had blown off the roof and the winter snow and moisture had finally caused it to give way. We were all gathered there for a meeting when it happened. Everyone stood with the 'where do we even start' stare. So we started all over again.

We had come from a church where people were encouraging and always patting us on the back for the tasks we would do. We got very spoiled. We weren't getting that pat here as much as I was used to and it was foreign to me. My husband spoke words of wisdom to me though. **"Honey if we want to be servants, we cannot have hurt feelings when we are treated like servants."**

With those words I held a good attitude for awhile, even doing my best, but pretty soon bitterness began to settle in. I began seething with anger every time I picked up a tipped over styrofoam cup under a pew laying next to a dried coffee stain or a wadded up tissue. Because of my anger, I knew in my heart and mind at this point that I was not even storing up blessings in heaven because of my heart attitude. So it was all for naught. As far as I was concerned it was a big waste of time.

I was falling into that trap we talked about earlier; the self-pity-I'm-a-victim-nobody-else-matters-it's-all-about-me trap. I felt that I was doing it all and nobody appreciated me. That wasn't true, but it is hard to see clearly when you are in the trap. I could not focus on the fact that I *should* be doing this for the Lord alone (**Colossians 3:23-24** - Whatever you do, work at it with all your heart, as working for the Lord, not for men, since you know that you will receive an inheritance from the Lord as a reward. It is the Lord Christ you are serving). I should not need a pat on the back, but I was stuck. I couldn't get a foothold to get out of the pit.

One Sunday we had visitors. It was the gentleman we had met at the first meeting and his wife. They had visited a couple of times. This man became a source of encouragement through different situations. He had seen how the church had grown from the eight people to sixty. He knew changes were happening. I had visited with his wife only briefly before. She was very quiet, but always encouraging. She was exactly who I needed to talk to this day. I approached her after church and told her I needed some advice. I could not control the tears. It seemed I was always on the verge of crying.

"I cannot figure out what my role is," I explained. "I feel that I am doing so many things that I cannot give 100% to anything."

She sympathized with me and said she understood. She proceeded to advise me, "What you need to do is make a list of the things you do. Pray over that list and then let God guide you to where He wants to use you. After you make that decision, then you let everyone else in the church know what you will be doing and it will be up to them to decide how the rest gets done."

Those words were so freeing to me. To hear another pastor's wife tell me that I did *not* have to be in charge of everything was such a relief. She shared with me that she felt called to work in the nursery so that is what she did.

I followed her instructions immediately after church and began praying over the list of things I was currently involved in. After deciding, I started letting the other women know what I would not be available to help with anymore. My husband and I wanted people to understand that this was their church and that they needed to be the ones to take care of it, to invest in it. Even though I was handing things over, I found it hard to let go of some things. Can anyone relate to that?

We did a Bible study one time and discussed the event where the friends of a certain man carried him on a mat and lowered him through the roof to be laid at the feet of Jesus (Mark 2). A very lengthy conversation took place regarding times when we have to be the ones carrying the mat versus times we need to be on the mat. As women, especially, I think it is hard for us to get on the mat and let others take care of us. We need to be needed and it can be scary when we feel we are not.

One woman asked, "What happens if we put the mat down and nobody picks the mat up again?"

Another joined in, "Or what if they do not pick up the mat like we would pick up the mat?"

At first it was a bit comical, but as the conversation progressed, it became evident that these were very real fears. We realized how much we like to control the situation.

 Some of the duties I was able to give up very easily. In fact, the woman who took over cleaning for me asked me one day, "I hope the cleaning has been being done up to your standard," to which I replied very quickly, "Honey, I've got no standard. I am just glad I don't have to do it." That felt good. I knew I had totally put that mat down.

Other things were not as easy. People were not picking up the mat like I would. I had to stop being so critical and realize that any effort should be appreciated. I went back and forth with some issues. Like I said, we need to be needed. I first experienced the panic that I was not needed when my first son was six years old and hanging out a lot more with Dallas. I felt excluded and complained that nobody needed me anymore.

"Of course we need you, Honey," he comforted. You know what's coming, don't you? "Who would do our laundry and make our dinner?" I knew he was just trying to be funny, but there was that moment of wondering what I would do if nobody needed me.

There was even a moment at the church. Dallas and I were gone for Christmas one year. The church family was having a New Year's Eve game night and one of the gals texted me and asked if I knew where something was. Just as I was getting ready to respond, she texted back and said that she had found the item. I quickly texted back "Need me."

She called laughing and said, "Of course we need you."

Occurance: Bitterness **Solution:** Put the mat down

7

INTERVIEW WITH A PASTOR'S WIFE

My aunt had once written me a letter with a great description of pastors' wives that she had known. She wrote:

> *"I got to thinking about how that role has evolved over my church experience. Years ago, our pastor's wife was a definite extension of him. She was lovely and dignified – always kind and sympathetic – quiet – reserved – pleasant- stood for everything her husband stood for – a perfect example of a pastor's wife. Then to my complete amazement, one day at a ladies meeting she said she probably would not have married him if she had known what her role would involve. Since then we have had such an array of strong, energetic, individual, working women who are pastors' wives, fulfilling their role as such,yet shining in their own light. They are musicians, speakers, missionaries, wives, mothers, teachers, friends – active in the community – strong women in their own right. Their love for the Lord and furthering of His kingdom are existent in all they do and say and yet they are individuals. Our pastor's wife now homeschools her children, one of whom is autistic, and that is her primary*

focus , as it should be. She is a partner to her husband but not to the point where church activities take priority over her mother role. And at this point in time, it's where she needs to put her efforts. So what if she doesn't accompany him on his visits or thinks she needs to be in the kitchen for everything. She has her priorities and I admire her for that and Pastor John totally supports her."

I loved that! I wish I would have went to my aunt when I first got out here. That description could have answered so many of my questions.

After reading that, I wondered how other pastors' wives viewed the ministry. Did they struggle? I came up with some questions to deliver to four women that I knew but with some hesitation. The women I was thinking of were all very classy women. They seemed to love being in the ministry and I certainly did not want to come across as disrespectful.

I took a chance and began by handing the questions to one woman at our church whose husband is a retired pastor (although I think he has more preaching engagements now than when he had his own church). I carefully explained the project I was working on and asked if she would want to participate. They only came to our church periodically so I did not know her very well. I was a little nervous about approaching her. She shocked me when she told me that she did not want to be a pastor's wife and when her husband came home and told her that he felt he was being called to preach she said, "No you are not!" I never would have suspected her reluctance by how she composes herself today.

I had another friend who was very new to the position. In fact, she and her husband began attending our church shortly after we came. After a period of time, we titled him our PIT (pastor in training) and he did many duties of an associate pastor. A church became available in a neighboring town and this couple was willing to say yes to God and step out of their comfort zone and preach the Word. I thought it would be interesting to see the difference, if any, in responses to the questions.

The next woman I chose has experienced many different levels of ministry. Her husband started as a pastor, but was moved into other roles of directing different programs in the association. This left her without a real church home as they traveled around a lot to take care of different churches. She said she would participate if she could remain anonymous. When she said that, I knew there were REAL feelings she would be sharing.

My final choice was a woman from a different denomination whose experience was very similar to mine. Her husband was not trained, but was called to preach. She became a great resource for me and she was safe for me to talk to and request her prayer support.

Some of the answers are very simple , others are lengthy, but they all come from the heart. The first thing that I noticed that we all had in common was the statement "many of the expectations placed on us came from ....us".

Interview Questions:

What surprised you most in your role as a ministry wife?

Dianne – I felt that people wanted me to fulfill areas I was not called to be in.

Donna – [I was surprised] that God chose me and my husband.

Mary – There was no real handbook! What surprised me the most in my role was the extremes of my feelings from being loved, and cared for, and then to being tied to the railroad tracks and left there alone.

Cyndi – [I was surprised by] the sheer magnitude of what we had decided to do in service to God. When we first started our ministry, our first one ever, I had a very limited idea of what my role would be. I thought my role would be to support my husband as the Pastor and that would be it, as it was an established church.

Well, I was both wrong and right. I have learned what the meaning of "support my husband as the Pastor" really means. It isn't just a "Hey honey, you're doing a great job" or "great message today" type of support. It's really having discussions with him about what is really going well, where some areas are that need addressed, and how can I help him. It's being there to shake him and say "You are doing a great job" and giving specific support for that; "Look at the new programs that are in place", "remember how great VBS turned out to be," "yes, that idea was great, but it didn't turn out so well; here's what we might want to do different."

It's also reminding him that the Lord put him there for a reason, even in, and especially in, the hard times. It is hard to walk into an established church, understand the culture, see where growth can be made, and implement that without totally alienating the rest of the congregation.

The other surprising thing was how willing the established members were to let you take over everything. You have to learn when to say "no" and what your limits are. You also have to learn how to delegate and how to assign people to be "in charge" of specific events so it all doesn't fall on you. Being a pastor's wife is both very trying and so very rewarding! I wouldn't change it!!

What was the most difficult about your role?

Dianne – Meeting everyone's expectations. I have to answer to God. Peace comes when we realize it is about Jesus, not all the others.

Donna – Discernment (the right thing to do and when) which comes from our Father above.

Mary – The most difficult part of being a minister's wife was trying to know and adjust to the many roles I felt people were expecting me to fulfill. Some of the roles: the perfect wife, mother, housekeeper, hostess and, of course, being the best dressed family in the church. Plus be able to transform into a trained, capable Bible teacher, musical genius and in some cases a janitor and yard keeper. After awhile most of these roles I realized were self imposed and the majority of the people loved the real me.

Cyndi – a. Learning what role the current congregation members want me to play and balancing that with changes that need to be made based on what the Lord is telling us in His word and through prayer. You have to figure out how to have those tough conversations in a way that builds people up and helps them to see the Biblical wisdom in your words.

b. The other difficult thing is learning when to give advice to your husband, the Pastor, and when to keep your mouth closed. You have to remember that you were not the one called to lead the congregation. He was. You have to remember that the Lord is guiding your husband, in the path he wants him to go. Sometimes the Lord will reveal that to you as well, but not always. You have to remember to submit to your husband, the Pastor, and let him lead your home as well. That can be a tough pill to swallow if you don't understand the Biblical foundation for it.

What was the hardest thing to adjust to?

Dianne – The loneliness as a pastor's wife.

Donna – Everyone calling my husband Pastor. Then there were those who just called him Wayne. I felt he deserved his respect like Dr. so and so. He was ordained so his real title was Reverend. I guess they could call him anything if it was in love.

Mary – The hardest thing to adjust to were the moves. On the average, we moved every two years, which meant new schools and friends for our two children. This was especially hard on our son who was the youngest and me because of my personality.

Cyndi - Learning to share my husband with the other members of the church was hard. It is amazing how much time is taken away from your "marriage time" once your husband is the Pastor. There is always someone who needs to vent, or needs advice, someone who has an emergency, or someone who just wants to talk with the pastor. Then there is the time they need to study and prepare for the Sunday message; and if he also teaches classes throughout the week, that is even more time gone from the "family & marriage" time. You have to learn to be very flexible and realize that you are the most "important" person in your husband's life, but the congregation and the issues surrounding them are the most "urgent".

What was the most rewarding in your role?

Dianne – Seeing people's lives become hungry for more of God and digging in and learning; Spiritual growth.

Donna – Teaching the 2 & 3 year olds and leading them to the Savior. The wordless book makes it very easy to lead them.

Mary - To see lost people come to know Jesus especially after years of praying and ministering to them then seeing them mature in their faith, including myself.

Cyndi - Seeing the growth in my husband as the pastor and seeing the deepening strength of our marriage through our relationship with the Father. It's amazing how the "last straw" issues of the past become an "opportunity for growth" as a couple when you are walking with the Lord. It is amazing and wonderful how your very core values and habits change as you deepen your roots with the Lord.

Knowing what you know now, if given the choice, would you go through it all again?

Dianne – Absolutely! It is worth it all!

Donna – I'm still going through it. Until I get to Glory. We might not get a salary anymore, but I can't live any other way. It's been 27 years already!

Mary - Yes, I would do it all again, but not set unreasonable expectations of myself. The other thing I wished I had realized early on was God's calling to the ministry wasn't just to my husband but to me also.

Cyndi - Absolutely! There are many things about this journey that have been difficult and trying,   but if we look at them for what they are- opportunities to grow with our Lord and obey His desires for us - how could you want it to be any other way?

Where did you feel God was wanting you to serve in the ministry?

Dianne – I have a strong knowing in my Spirit that God has placed me here to minister to women.

Donna – My family was first and helps. My husband and I visited people together for salvation or just to talk. Praying is high on the list of servitude.

Mary - I feel God gifted me to serve in the 'behind the scenes' ministries, which included children's church, nursery worker, home-bound, and kitchen hostess. These are usually the hardest ministries to fill, but I served there with a joyful heart.

Cyndi - I believe that one of the gifts the Lord has given me is the gift of Teaching. I knew from the first day we stepped into our church that I was there to be a teacher of the Word to the children. My other gift from God is compassion for those in need. There are always members of the congregation, members of the church or not, who need you to be there for them no matter what. They need you to listen, to possibly give advice in a way that gives them hope and direction, and they need to know that you, and most importantly that the Lord, love them and want to have that relationship with them no matter how tattered their past, present, or future may be. People need to be inspired by the love, grace, and mercy of our Father; sometimes on a daily basis. Being able to help people experience the love of God and helping them access and grow in their relationship with God makes everything else worthwhile.

What did the church people expect you to be?

Dianne – Perfect (and I'm only human).

Donna – I thought to be everything to everybody, but in truth, just to be the Christian woman God wanted me to be.

Mary - Mary referred back to the second question for this answer (Some of the roles: the perfect wife, mother, housekeeper, hostess and, of course, being the best dressed family in the church. Plus be able to transform into a trained, capable Bible teacher, musical genius and in some cases a janitor and yard keeper. But after a while most of these roles I realized were self imposed and the majority of the people loved the real me.)

Cyndi - I think it was a learning curve for all of us. We've basically waded our way through to where we are right now. The role has morphed over time and I think we are in a good place. I just have to remember to delegate so I don't overwhelm myself. I think the ladies of the church and I work well together to organize events for our youth, for the multiple congregations (we have a Spanish Mission in our church as well), and for the community. It definitely has to be a "team" mentality.

What did your husband, as Pastor, expect from you?

Dianne – I felt he wanted perfection, but realized I brought those thoughts on myself. He just wanted me to be there for him and a lot of times to be still; not to do or say anything, just pray.

Donna – My love for him, family and church family. He wanted me to be one that he could confide in.

Mary - My husband has always been supportive of me, and the ministries I felt God wanted me to be involved in. He always told the church where I chose to serve was between God and me. The only public thing he asked of me was to stand with him at the door when the services were over so I could visit with people as they left church. This was always a high point for me and people would often share prayer requests, burdens and joys with me.

Cyndi - This too, I think has morphed over time. As we both sort of walked into this blind, we have learned what we needed, and continue to need, from each other in this journey as we go along. It continues to be an ever growing and changing process. I think if we become stagnant in our ability to read each other and ask for help, then we will start to experience some struggles. I do think he needs me to help him organizationally; mostly because of all of the different directions he is pulled as the pastor, at any given moment.

What boundaries, if any, did you have to set?

Dianne – The only boundaries I set were for my spiritual growth.

Donna – Forbid gossip!!

Mary - I had to set boundaries to protect my children from any issues or problems that might be happening in the church. I also set boundaries on what personal information, like health or family concerns, I would share with people in the church. There were times when I shared personal concerns asking for confidence and then have other church members ask me about them. In looking back I wish I had set boundaries with church members regarding no interruptions at meal times, as well as the days my husband had set aside to spend with family except, of course, in emergencies.

Was it easy to connect to other pastors' wives?

Dianne – Not really. A person gets too busy in their own churches and world of ministries. I do pray for other pastors' wives. I feel compassion and love for them.

Mary - I didn't have many opportunities to connect with other pastors' wives. For most of our ministry I worked full time outside the home, from the time my children were in diapers until they finished school and left home. I did this to support the family while my husband completed his education. Then we started pastoring a church where our denomination was not strong. Hence the salary package was small, which required my employment to supplement our income. In my husband's last two pastorates I did not have to work, but found most other pastors' wives in the same position I was early on in the ministry. In my husband's present ministry there is some connection, but early on, the perception was I would come in and lead women's Bible studies, give talks, etc. but that is not my calling or gift.

Any other thoughts?

Dianne- Prayer and seeking out God's plan for Pastor and I as a couple and for the flock God placed us here to lead is so important. He equips us to do the job.

Donna – I needed to always think before saying something that could hurt someone or damage our ministry. It's truly OUR ministry (service) together helping where we can. Our Wonderful God and Savior is SO worthy of our love and service.

Cyndi - I think we, as the pastors' wives, have to remember to be the earthly rock and foundation for our husbands and remember that God planned for us to be in this position as well. God is depending on us, and expecting us to support our husbands in this journey so that our husbands can, in turn support the rest of the flock. We must be the physical and emotional support system, the voice of reason, the safe place to hide, and the cheerleader of cheerleaders. Our husbands have to know and believe that we support them 100% no matter what. Things are never perfect, but if we trust in our Lord and let Him lead our path, we can get pretty darn close.

I am so thankful for each one of these women. I have a deep respect for each one and appreciate them being transparent with this interview. They put many things into words that I was having a hard time conveying. Some of their statements made me want to cry. I could feel the hurt and loneliness that they were talking about, but I loved how they would bring it back around to God and understanding that this is where we have each been called to be. We have a job to do. When we talk about choices in our Bible studies, we often bring up Jonah and determine that we can get there clean or we can get there pukey, but we are going to get there. When we finally make the choice to surrender to God, we realize it is a much easier journey if we decide to get there clean.

8
COUNT THE COST

Backing up to our first year at the church; we had so much to learn. Not only did we have to delve into the business side of church, but we also had to face many trials that could have made us wonder if it was worth it.

Dallas and I each claim not to be a real people person. We are homebodies and have never been big on exercising hospitality. So the first thing we had to learn, of course, was how to handle calls coming in at all hours of the day and night and people stopping by unannounced. It wasn't a horrible thing. It just took some getting used to, but it did not take too long for us to figure out a system and know when things could be handled later or if they were urgent.

When the tables were turned, it took the people from the church time to get used to us setting boundaries. There were times when they would want us to drop what we were doing and deal with issues that could not be dealt with until the next day anyway. We did all learn to get along and we loved everybody to pieces, but we loved like earthly brothers and sisters and did not always see eye to eye.

There was another aspect that I struggled with, more so than my husband. I have always considered myself a very private person. I do not want people knowing my business especially my family business. I have always been that way. Now I felt like our life was an open book. I felt that every move I made was being critiqued. This was more something I laid on myself than anybody else did. We did have a group of pretty down to earth people and I learned who I could truly be myself with and who I had to be guarded in front of.

The following is a poem written by one of the young women in the congregation, the same one who challenged me to write the earlier poem, I Am a Pastor's Wife.

THE PASTOR'S WIFE

With ankles crossed
and hands placed neatly in her lap;
Her hair is pinned back,
not a piece out of place;
Her Sunday dress
seven days a week;
A smile as sweet as honey
and her voice never rose.
Thankfully,
This is not my Pastor's wife.
Her smile is sweet,
always real,
but not constantly there.
Her Sunday dress
disappears by 2 p.m.
if even worn at all.
Her hair pinned back,
long and curly
and sometimes untamed.
Thank the Lord,
for the Pastor's wife
I have.

Kimbre Adams
10/2/11

Many of the women in the church were thankful that I was a "real" person, but I have had people bluntly tell me what my job was, to whom I would apologize and thank them for reminding me what I should be doing. Although it would upset me momentarily, I would try to learn from it.

I learned to be very perceptive. I learned that some people expected me to read their minds. It was easy to know what was needed by the people that I would see every week. It would take a little longer for me to figure out what new people needed from me or ones that only came periodically, if I caught it at all. That is usually when I would be in trouble. One sad thing I learned was that I could not be real in front of everybody.

At one point it caused sort of an identity crisis. Who was I? I knew what my children expected of me and I knew what my husband expected me to be. I even knew what EACH individual person in the church expected from me, but who was *I*.

Dallas handled it so much better than I did. I'm not sure if that was just his personality or because he was a man. He didn't care who thought what. He had the "what you see is what you get" attitude which I craved to have. One of my sons was the same way. His attitude was one of, "If you don't like me, don't hang out with me, but this is who I am."

I was just too much of a people pleaser. I did not like that about myself. I always wanted people to like me and I found out very quickly, and had to come to terms with the fact, that some people were going to like me and some people weren't and they would make every effort to make sure I knew it. I got used to it and was able to shrug it off for the most part. I had to realize it was not me that they were rejecting.

We pushed forward through these learning experiences and things started to simmer down a bit, but the devil was sitting right around the corner waiting to punch us in the nose. Never let your guard down.

It was September of 2006 and I had just received word that my dad was in the hospital from a heart attack, his second. I was so distraught and now felt the weight of being so far away. My brothers and Mom told me there was no need for me to come home, that he was okay, but I felt like a deserter to my family. It made my heart ache to know that both of my younger brothers were close enough to be there and support Mom and I was so far away. We were in a poor way financially and I didn't know what to do. When the people from the church found out about it, they took a love offering and sent me on my way. It was just me and our two youngest boys, Christopher and Eli, heading out on a 17 hour trip. Dallas thought it was best that he stay home since there wasn't really anyone at the church to take his place at that time. I had to get used to traveling alone for this reason.

I spent ten days with my family and left knowing that my dad was, in fact, going to be okay. I felt good as we headed home and was anxious to get back. I knew by the time I got back that my new daughter-in-law would be there as our son had just left to Iraq and she would be staying with us. I was ready to get back into a routine with church and homeschooling. Little did I know at that moment that in four days after my return, my routine would be disturbed for a long time.

On that fourth day, I took Christopher and Eli into the city for some state testing that they had to do for school. We headed back to the house about 4:00 PM. The boys were in good moods so I thought since Dallas was working a side job and wouldn't be home until later, we would stop at our classroom and do a bit of school work. We actually used a classroom in the basement of the old Assembly of God Church, one block north of our house. There were four other moms who had classrooms down there also.

The boys had been in the middle of some activities when my cell phone rang. I answered it and it went dead. I never could get very good reception in the basement. It rang again and once more I tried to answer it. The same thing happened. I saw that it was my daughter-in-law. I knew I would be going home in half an hour so figured I would just catch up with her then.

Just as I closed the phone, it rang a third time. It was my son calling from South Dakota. I answered and his voice came through very clear…and very calm.

He asked, "Mom, is our house on fire?"

"That's not funny, JJ," I laughed.

"Mom, I'm not trying to be funny. I need you to tell me if our house is on fire," he repeated with no hint of foolery in his voice.

"No, it's not," I replied trying to figure out what he was trying to pull.

"Are you *at* the house?" He was keeping his voice so steady. So calm.

"….No," I hesitated then quickly came back with, "How would you know anyway, you're in South Dakota?"

"I'm on MySpace with my friend (who lived two doors down from us) and she said the house is on fire. Will you please go check," this was not a question.

With it still not sinking in and just to appease him I said, "Fine, I'll go check and call you right back." I told Christopher and Eli to stay in the room. I knew I would be able to see our house from the front of the building. I walked down the hallway and through the kitchen. I turned right and opened the front door.

At that moment, coming down the cement steps was one of my friends, another homeschooling mom. She looked at me and quietly asked, "Are your boys here?" No words would come out of my mouth. I studied her solemn face as I nodded yes. She gently said, "You need to go." She covered her mouth with her hand as I moved past her through the dark stairwell in what seemed like slow motion.

As I neared the corner of the street cautiously, I looked in the direction of my house and the first thing I saw was the thick, black plume of smoke rising from a hole in the roof of my house, right over my bedroom. My legs were numb yet they were able to move in a sprint. I did not know what was more deafening, the sirens of the fire trucks already on the scene, my heart pounding, or the sound of my voice as I heard it scream in rapid succession, "No, no, no, no, no, no, NO! NO! NO!" I ran into my front yard as one of the female fire volunteers stopped me and told me I could not go in.

The first people I saw as I turned around were my friends, Diane and her husband. The pastor approached me and the first sentence out of my mouth was "What does He want from me!" as I shook my fist toward heaven. In my head, or maybe out loud, it was hard to tell, I tried to reason it out by saying, "My dad just had a heart attack and now You want my *house*?! We are doing *Your* work for *Your* Kingdom, what else do You want from me?" I hugged Diane and whispered in an exhausted voice, "I do not have time for this."

Then there were swarms of people around me. My daughter-in-law came out from the neighbor's house. She said she had been taking a nap. She woke up thinking she smelled smoke and went into our bedroom which was already on fire. (We found out later it started from a faulty bathroom fan.) She got herself and our two dachshunds out with their puppies. When she could not get a hold of me, she called Dallas at work. He was on his way. My neighbor lady came up to me and took hold of my shoulders until I would focus on her and said, "People are bringing some items for you," she motioned to a small box of blankets behind me and continued. "But you have to make up a needs list so we can get it in the paper for you."Then I broke down. I cried, "I'm *tired* of being in need. I was just IN need. I don't want to be in need again."

She boldly replied, "But you are and you need to let people help you." It was my turn to be on the mat.

Dallas arrived and quickly began wandering around to see who could give him some answers. I turned and saw that the box of blankets had turned into a small mountain of pillows, coats, new toothbrushes, shampoo, soap and even dog food. I was overwhelmed with the thought people were putting into the items they were bringing. I started loading things into the car.

Diane and her husband gave us $100 and a key to an empty double wide they had available a couple of blocks straight up the street, past our school. We stood in the street until 11:00 PM when the firefighters were completely finished with their work. They walked us through the house to see the damage at which time Dallas immediately discovered our Bibles and grabbed them. A couple of friends took us out for a bite to eat before we came back and settled into our temporary home.

That night, as I struggled with my own emotions, I also struggled with my husband's emotions. He was not acting like we had just had our house burn down. He was smiling and trying to joke. I did not understand it. When I confronted him, he explained, "If I start crying over this, I may not stop. The things we lost are just that – things. **Everything that makes a house a home is right here in this room – us. We need to understand that this is a chance for us to be a witness. Everybody, especially those at the church, are going to be watching to see how we deal with this situation."**

 Why did he always have to make sense? Why couldn't he just let me wallow in my muck and mire? He was right, of course. We did lose all of the furniture, but this community was so awesome. We had a FULLY furnished house within five days without spending a dime. In fact, before the fire, we didn't have a micro-wave. After the fire, we had seven offered to us. We literally had to start turning things away because we had no need for them.

We were able to save everything from our daughter's bed-room; the only room that didn't have any damage at all. Ironical-ly, Desire's bedroom was completely decorated with fireman knickknacks, framed fire truck puzzles, stuffed animals dressed like firemen and more. Her dream was to one day fight fires.

I took my husband's words to heart and worked hard at help-ing to clean and save what we could from the house. It felt good to be in control in such an uncontrollable situation. The pastor from First Baptist Church asked me at the end of the week in a sympathetic voice, "JoEllen, how are you feeling?"

"Victorious," I sighed with a smile. The look on his face matched what was on my mind. Surprise. The word came out so automatically, I was not even sure who had said it.

"Really?" he asked.

Then I straightened up as it sank in. "Yes, This is *my* victory. Does the devil not know who he is dealing with? I am royalty, Baby! I am daughter of the King Most High and this is MY victo-ry!"

Even through the *years* of transition, going from house to house to fifth wheel to house, God was faithful and I learned, like Dallas told me the night of the fire, that material things don't mat-ter. Relationships matter. Our family matters. Keeping our faith in God matters. Material things just don't matter.

A young girl at our church once told me that "God is God when we're way up here (holding her hand above her head) and God is God when we're way down here (moving her hand down to mid thigh). She was right. This was a time we just had to know in our knowers that God was in control and His ways were higher than ours.

I thought later about how good God was through it all and I was so thankful that I served a God who was big enough to handle my anger. I saw how He had protected me from my daughter-in-law's call as I listened to her frantic messages later. Instead, God used my son to calmly walk me through what I had to do. Isn't it awesome to know that our Father knows His children so well that He understands what each one will respond to and what each one can handle?

Now, of course, I am not saying that your house will burn down if you go into the ministry, but rather that there will be a cost involved. God may never ask anything drastic, but wants to know you are willing to do what it takes to serve Him.

The cost that we have to pay will still be used by God. Some situations I found myself going through I feel were allowed by God so that when I came across other people dealing with those same issues, I could truly relate to their heartaches and fears. I could help them find the light in the dark room that they found themselves in.

For example, shortly after our fire, another friend of mine had a house fire. I knew what she was in need of physically and mentally.

I went through a short bout of depression and only a couple months afterwards a gentleman was in our church sharing that his wife struggled with depression. I was able to encourage him to be patient with her and love her through it.

I went through an irrational time of loneliness (it seems irrational now, but at the time it was very real). Two months afterward, God brought a young couple into the church. The wife was so lonely. I just wanted to hug her because I knew how she ached inside.

I had experienced post partum depression with my last birth so I am careful to keep my eyes and ears open to the new moms and watch for signs of that trial.

I am convinced God gave me a taste of these heartaches to give me a deeper compassion and understanding. (**II Corinthians 1:4** - He comforts us in all our tribulation, that we may be able to comfort them who are in any trouble, by the comfort with which we ourselves are comforted of God).

Occurrence:
Invasion

Solution:
Discernment and
setting boundaries

Occurrence:
Trials

Solution:
Rejoice in the opportu-
nities to witness
through the storms

Heart Condition:
Depressed

9
MASKS

Victory was mine after the fire, but I let go of it. I am not sure at what point I let go, but I did. I tend to do that. I started slipping into a depression. I was getting jealous over silly things. I started to spiral out of control. My husband was willing to do anything he could to help me. I tried to keep the communication open with him and tried to explain everything I was feeling and going through but I started taking it too far.

In this turmoil, I felt that I had to put on a mask when I went out in public and pretend that everything was okay. Because I did not want everybody knowing my business, I wouldn't go talk to anybody about it. I was condemning myself, "I am a grounded Christian. How can *I* be dealing with depression?" The only time I took the mask off was when I came home and I think Dallas wished I would have kept it on there many times too.

I couldn't pray. I couldn't think. For three months I cried every day. My mind did not *want* to be depressed. I didn't know if it was my body's reaction to the trauma of the fire or what. I had taken the kids to the school one day and a friend stopped in to say hi. She smiled and said, "So, how are you doing?"

I was so thankful I had remembered my mask before I left the house that day. "I'm doing great! We are getting school done during the day. Pastor Phil said we can stay in the house behind the First Baptist Church until June. Everything is moving right along!"

Then she threw me for a loop. See, most people would have bought that answer. Not her. She nodded and smiled as I talked and then said, "Great!" She pulled up a chair and lost the smile. "So how are you really doing?"

Oh no! *Had* I forgotten my mask?! I was sure I put it on! What happened? I buried my face in my hands and sobbed. I shook my head. She dismissed Christopher and Eli to go play for a while. When they were out of the room, I raised my head and looked at her and whispered, "This sucks! I hate this! I hate moving and living out of boxes and not knowing when things are going to be normal again. *Are* things going to be normal again? I hate this! I can't quit crying. I've been jealous like some 16 year school girl. I don't know what's wrong with me!" She listened and just let me cry. It did feel good to get it out to somebody.

Having people in your life that you can trust is a must; people that you *can* be transparent with. Our husbands should be the first ones we can go to with everything, but even most of them will admit they would rather you have a girlfriend to cry to. Emotions and men just don't seem to mix real well. Our husbands may be willing to try, but remember, this is a lot to lay on them.

Having women you can pair up with to be a prayer partner is also important. If at all possible, have someone outside the church that you can go to. We want to protect the flock as much as we can. They come in looking for stability, thinking that we have it figured out and it can make them a little nervous when they know that we struggle.

There are many women I know that will pray for me, but only a few that are perceptive enough to know WHEN I am in need of prayer. It is still hard for me to ask for prayer on certain things.

I remember one time in particular. Our phone rang at 5:00 AM. The mother of a young couple from our church informed us that they had lost their one day old baby girl. We immediately went over and spent time with the family.

That same day I went into town to see a friend of mine. She told me that her sister, whose healing from cancer we had been praying for, had passed away. As I was leaving, my cell phone rang. It was another woman from our church, saying her sister had just been diagnosed with cancer. I didn't understand what was happening that day; so much heartache. I drove home, emotionally exhausted and my husband met me at the door and said, "Honey, Amy called. She is upset after hearing about the baby. Can you call her?" Amy was one of the younger members of our church, about 16 years my junior, very spiritually wise for a girl her age though.

I walked down to the church to use the office phone and tried to pull myself together before even trying to call. I took some deep breaths so I could keep control of my voice. I dialed her number and she answered quickly. "Hi, Amy. It's Jo. Dallas said you called. Are you alright?"

With complete compassion in her young voice, "Jo, are *you* okay? This cannot be easy for you to deal with."

"No," was all I could say, the tears automatically flowing.

"Father, I just ask right now that you comfort JoEllen......" Amy <u>immediately</u> started praying over me. There was no hesitation. She was thoughtful enough to know that the baby's family was probably surrounded by family and friends, but she made me realize through her actions that we do not think about the people who are doing the ministering *to* these families in need. It takes a lot of strength and energy. It drains you as you try to be everything they need you to be at that time; a strong shoulder, a listening ear, words of wisdom, understanding, organizational skills, a compassionate heart.

With that experience I learned that I needed to be more perceptive. I needed to watch and try to see past the masks that others wore when they came into the church. I learned that I could pray right then and there for somebody, not just voice the words, "I will be praying for you." I also learned who to go to when I was in need of prayer.

I have learned to allow people into my world, to be transparent. It is a scary place to be and you do run the risk of being judged, but as far as your overall mental health, it is worth the risk.

Even if we are too prideful to go ask for prayer, God has His ways of encouraging us. I was going through a stage when I just wanted to hear the words , "I am praying for you." I KNEW people were praying for me. I didn't doubt that at all, but I needed to HEAR it. God provided.

Chris, Eli and I were in the city one day. I ran into construction and got lost. I figured I would wind my way through a subdivision that was in the direction I needed to go and hoped it had an outlet on the other side. It did and I found myself at a familiar stop light. It was right down from my friend's house so I told the boys we would stop by and see her. We made our way there and I went up and knocked on the door. The door was whisked open and the screen door pushed out. There stood my friend, still in pajamas and hair all a muss. I had never seen her like that before. "Come in, come in! I was just praying for you!"

She continued to rant about how God had told her there were some words I was needing to hear as she bustled around the living room like a bumble bee trying to figure out which flower it would land on next. "It's in one of these notebooks," she said. I could barely make out what she was saying because I was still stuck on the fact that God let me hear the words I had been longing for. She found the notebook and located the scribble that belonged to me. "Here it is! God said that you need to stop looking for others to fit in with, that He is the only One you need to look to. *I don't know what it means. I hope you do.*" She seemed to be rambling a million words a minute.

"Yes, I know what it means." I knew that I needed to stop looking for approval and acceptance in the other pastors' wives and just go to God and figure out what I needed to do.

After leaving, I drove to the post office to check our mail box. There was a small white envelope with beautiful handwriting on it so I knew it was a personal letter. I looked at the return address and when I didn't recognize the name, I looked at the state from which it came. It had arrived from Oklahoma. I didn't know anybody in Oklahoma and was even more curious because my name was spelled correctly, a rarity, especially from people I didn't know. In my curiosity, I opened it as soon as I got into the car. Inside was a card with butterflies on the front dancing around summer flowers. I lifted the top of the card up and read these words:

Dear JoEllen,
I know you do not know me, but I have been praying for you. God wants you to know that you are the apple of His eye.

I stopped right there and bowed my head in prayer, "You overwhelm me, Father. Why do you bless me? You are so good! Thank You!" I smiled when I saw the mailing label. The day I received it was November 23 and the date it showed it was mailed was mid-October. It seemed like God had held it in the post office until the very day that I needed to hear those words. God will do those sorts of things to keep His daughters encouraged.

Occurrence:
Wearing masks

Solution:
Find a friend
you can be
transparent
with

Occurrence:
Tough times

Solution:
Find a prayer partner

10
A CHANGE OF HEART

In December of 2010 I made up my mind that things were going to be different this year. *I* was going to be different. It was my New Year's resolution, you might say. God had energized me. The Holy Spirit was stirred up inside of me. I knew that I could only change with the Lord's help.

I realized God was giving me a second chance, one I didn't deserve. I saw all of the time that I had wasted this first five years. I was tired of being bitter and angry and depressed. I knew I needed to pull it together. Thankfully, God did still use me for His purpose. **Isaiah 14:24** tells us that God's plan will not be frustrated. The first time I heard that verse, I thought the teacher had said God's plan will not be frustrat<u>ing</u>. I was the first to beg to differ on *that* point. Then she corrected me.

It was my heart condition that kept me from seeing the things God was doing all around me. Pride had formed a deep chasm in my heart inviting Judgment and Jealousy to try to fill it. They, in turn, wanted to spread the word about the little party they were having so they had their friends, Depression and Self Centeredness, join in the fun. Before I knew it, they had control and, as in any heart disease, it started effecting the rest of my world. This is what I read in an eHow Health article:

"Each type of heart disease shares one trait. It ultimately hinders this organ's life-giving pumping ability. Without proper medical attention, heart disease can eventually cause a potentially fatal heart attack.

I was on the verge of a spiritual heart attack! I knew the Good Doctor. I knew where the medicine was and I was rejecting it. The article goes on to say:

"The GOOD NEWS is that effective treatments and lifestyle modifications are enabling many individuals to successfully manage heart disease."

The Good News *is* the medicine. The Good News of the Gospel was going to be the only effective treatment that would get me on the road to good health, but I would have to make the conscious effort of making those lifestyle modifications so that I could manage the heart disease.

We are all born with the same heart disease and that is sin. We have to learn to manage it. **Genesis 4:6-7** says, "If you do what is right, will you not be accepted? But if you do not do what is right, sin is crouching at your door; it desires to have you, but you must master it." Again, it is a choice. We can master sin. In fact, I looked up the definition of the word crouch. One of the definitions was: ready to pounce. The one definition I liked was: cowering in fear. If we do what is right, sin will be cowering in fear at our presence.

I had to start by asking God to cleanse my heart. I asked Him to start revealing things to me that I needed to deal with. He was faithful, as always, and revealed to me the morning after that prayer three things I needed to be cleansed from; things that I didn't even realize were still in my heart. There was anger and bitterness and unforgiveness that He had put me on task to deal with first. I continued asking God to cleanse me and I would deal with those items as He brought them in front of me. I was glad He only gave me a few at a time because I would have gotten completely overwhelmed if He had given it to me all at once, but He knew that.

So I went into 2011 *wanting* to be happy. I knew that nobody could steal my joy, *nobody*, but I wanted that joy to surface. I wanted to reveal on the outside what I had on the inside. My husband tried teaching me a long time ago that I am the only one in charge of my happiness. I am in charge of my actions and reactions no matter what my circumstances. Paul said he had learned to be content in every situation. **(Philippians 4:11-13** - I am not saying this because I am in need, for I have learned to be content whatever the circumstances. I know what it is to be in need and I know what it is to have plenty, I have learned the secret of being content in any and every situation, whether well fed or hungry, whether living in plenty or in want. I can do all things through Christ who gives me strength). So it can be done. It's a choice.

I had to come to a point where I stopped playing the blame game and took some responsibility for my life. When I stopped playing the victim, it was easier to see (and help) others who were in that self-pity-I'm-a-victim-nobody-else-matters-it's-all-about-me trap. The purpose was two-fold when I came across other people in this trap; one, I was able to relate to them and give them some tools to help them through it and two, it forced me to see what I looked like to other people. It embarrassed me. I was so ashamed of the way I had acted and the turmoil I had put my husband and children through.

A friend and I were visiting one day and she shared with me that perky people annoyed her and wondered if it was because she was so unhappy. Her chin quivered with emotion. It broke my heart. I knew exactly what she was going through. It took me a long time to rejoice when others were happy or when good things happened to them. I was a Christian woman but fought the battle of jealousy on so many levels. I had to make a conscious effort to say "I am so excited for you" instead of "Why can't those sorts of things happen to me?"

So as the Holy Spirit performed heart surgery on me and I began to recover from years of self sabotage, I found myself WANTING to help at the church more. I WANTED to clean the church because I wanted those who walked through the door to be blessed. I WANTED to get out of my comfort zone and help others in their ministries if help was needed. I WANTED to help with teaching classes again. I was willing to take on the women's ministry events planning, which was very much out of my comfort zone.

As God saw that I was willing, He slowly started to stretch me. Each time I could feel that stretch, I would try to wriggle my way out with thoughts of panic, but He would prove Himself faithful....again and assure me that He was the one planning it all. I don't consider myself a very creative person . . . . like at all. That is something that does not come easily to me, but God was flooding me with ideas. Sometimes He would give them to me at the last minute, but one thing I have learned about our Father is that He is the God of perfect timing. He NEVER let me down.

What boggled me was that I could not figure out why I was surprised every time a prayer was answered when I asked for help on ideas. Isn't that funny? We claim to serve a big God. We tell everyone how great He is. Then when He blesses us, we're surprised. Shouldn't we expect great blessings from a great God?

So that makes me wonder; do we not feel worthy of His blessings or do we not believe what we tell others about Him? Are we sold hook, line and sinker, as my husband would say? Do we know why we believe what we believe? Do we believe **Jeremiah**

29:11 that reveals God's heart when He says "For I know the plans I have for you," declares the Lord, "plans to prosper you and not to harm you, plans to give you hope and a future"? Our Father wants nothing more than to bless His children.

My kids were all in the room one day picking on each other and I noticed what great smiles they had. Their laughter was so genuine and from the heart. I found myself wanting to do things or say things that would make them smile so I could see it one more time. Do you think it is that way for our Heavenly Father also? I do. I just giggle with some of the blessings He pours down on me because I know He is doing it just so He can see me smile one more time.

Occurrence: Needing to renew your Spirit **Solution:** Ask God for cleansing and consent to heart surgery	**Occurrence:** Overcoming negativity **Solution:** Make a choice

11
BLESSINGS UPON BLESSINGS

The things I noticed immediately after I made the decision to change my heart were the blessings and "open doors" that God laid before me. By immediately, I mean THE DAY I spoke the words "Lord, I surrender".

That very day my husband shared with me that he wanted to get the church focused back on prayer. He had been evaluating the last year at the church and trying to determine the point when people's attitudes changed and saw that it happened when we stopped praying as much.

We used to be very diligent in spending the last half hour or more of our Bible studies or Sunday school having everybody take a turn praying. Somewhere along the line we started getting in a hurry and would just close with a quick prayer. Since the connection was revealed to him, Dallas said, "I am going to share with the church that we need to get back on our knees and I am going to start by challenging the leaders to pray with their wives." Prayer answered! I had longed to pray with my husband! We would pray in front of each other in church and in classes, but we had never done it with just the two of us.

It actually sounds very strange when I say that out loud to people, that a pastor and his wife didn't pray together, but after asking other pastors about the subject, we weren't alone.

It was awkward at first because that had always been such a private thing in our individual walk with God. My husband has always explained to people that just when he thinks our marriage is the best it can be, God takes it to that next level. Well, it happened again. We thought we were doing great, but when we committed to praying together every night, I think we jumped up five levels! It was so incredible how much more we connected in every aspect of our marriage. I always knew my husband prayed for me, but to hear him pray OVER me each night melted my heart. To actually hear the love and adoration he had for me pouring out of his heart was beyond overwhelming. There were also times in his prayers that he would say something that I would want to take offense to, but when I asked myself if it was truth, and it generally was, I knew that God was speaking directly through him. We both realized that this was probably the single most important decision we had ever made in our marriage.

Another blessing came shortly after as I began to plan a Valentine's Party at the church geared towards community kids. I had never planned anything like it before, but God gave me the courage and the ideas to make it come to pass. The ladies of the church were a huge help and we had a lot of kids come through the door. We were very encouraged and excited. Next we planned a luncheon for St. Patrick's Day, again offered to the community and had a small group of people come, but it was still people from outside the church and that was what we wanted.

We had been praying for God to bring the lost and the broken to our church and for workers. We desperately needed workers. In January the Lord brought us a young family who wanted so badly to be a part of a church family. They wanted to jump right in and help with activities and events. We were very thankful and loved watching this family grow. Anything we suggested they do, they did. We suggested praying as a couple and praying as a family. They did. We suggested having family time in the Bible, they did and they grew.

Many times people would come to Dallas for advice, but were never willing to follow it and then complained that they were not growing spiritually. There were also times people would ask him for his opinion on an issue in their life and he would speak Truth to them and they would leave the church. Dallas knew they just wanted him to tickle their ears. So to have a family come in so eager to learn, to grow and to help was extremely refreshing.

We then had another middle aged couple come on a Sunday. I introduced myself to the tall, thin woman with shoulder length, brown hair styled with bangs that hung right below her eyebrows. She had a soft smile that matched her soft voice. She shook my hand and said "My name is Debbie. My husband and I are traveling and will be at the campground down the road for four weeks. Where can we be used?" Wow! Another blessing. So I didn't hold back. I shared with her the events that were happening during those four weeks and encouraged them to come and be a part. Then she informed me that she sang and would love to put on a little concert to bless us. We arranged to have her do that. Her songs were originals and very uplifting. She sang with such energy, you couldn't help but smile. God was just blessing us left and right with good hearted people. `

As we came upon the Easter season, we geared up for the annual Last Days of Jesus play that we participate in with the First Baptist Church. My husband was asked to play the part of Jesus. We immediately started praying protection over Dallas and over our marriage. We have seen the people that have played that role in the past come under some heavy attack. Dallas was no exception.

A gentleman walked into our church during this time and had a large family and was very enthusiastic. He asked Dallas if he could get involved. He immediately wanted to start teaching the adult classes and his boldness put Dallas on guard. Dallas told him he would very much like to get to know him and have him start attending Sunday school and meet the other people. Then one day at coffee this gentleman told Dallas that he was feeling pulled out to our church.

Dallas assured him, "Of course you are because my wife and I have been praying for workers."

The man responded with, "No, God told me I am to come out here and take your place."

Calmly Dallas stated, "Well, you're not the only one God speaks to and He has told me to stay the course."

With everything going on at the time and with the mental stress of the Easter play, Dallas could have very easily allowed doubt to come in and convince him that he was not the one to be preaching. He could have used this as his way out of the ministry. Six months before that he was asking the Lord if he had taken this church as far as he could and if it was time for someone else to take over, but the only message that kept coming was "Stay the course. Stay the course."

It didn't surprise me that Dallas was asking God this question. It was not the first time. He just wanted to make sure that he was in the Lord's will. I am glad Dallas has the gift of discernment because he could have taken this man so boldly walking in as his "sign".

Being a pastor of a small country church, we were not rolling in the money and many times my husband would work side jobs. Let me set something straight though. I took a spiritual gift test and poverty came up as my number one gift. I took great pride in calling my parents and telling them, "See, I'm not poor, I'm gifted!"

Dallas had worked with one of the builders in the church, but things had slowed down for him for a period of time. At the beginning of summer, our friend's son offered Dallas a job irrigating his fields. It was something he had never done before, but he had always secretly wanted to be a farmer. He told the young man he would give it a try. He did and he loved it. Being outdoors was his thing anyway. He learned very quickly how to do the siphon tubes and moved his way up to the wheel lines and gating pipe. He figured he would be done with it all come November, but they wanted to keep him around for chopping the fields and mechanic work. He took our younger boys out to work with him and they all learned how to work together as a team. Dallas loved the bonding time.

Because of the extra money being earned through this job, we were able to get back into Civil War re-enacting, a hobby Dallas and our older boys used to do together. Eli had always been too little so he and I had only been on one other one. Since he was old enough now, we decided to get back into it for the sake of Chris and Eli. What a great time we had, dressing up in Civil War gear, camping in canvas tents, performing battles and camp duties and just really escaping from reality. Mind you, this is coming from a non-camper and I really was blessed. I met a new family that summer that also homeschooled. The wife and I really seemed to click.

The first re-enactment we went to that summer was in Spokane, WA and when Sunday came we attended chapel service at which time the chaplain said that this would be his last re-enactment and there would be an opening for a preacher. The captain of our unit tried to get Dallas to sign up for the position, but Dallas reminded him that he came to these events to get away from preaching. We saw God's provision when this new family joined our unit and said they were evangelists. The gentleman was very nervous and felt that there was a big difference between evangelizing and preaching. It was fun to watch Dallas sit down with him and give him pointers and encourage him. It was also exciting for me to relive those first time emotions with his wife as she prayed that her husband would succeed in his new task.

When his first Sunday came to preach at the Port Gamble, Washington re-enactment I could tell she was trying not to hold her breath the entire time he was speaking. The tension released in tears at the end of the sermon as she expressed how proud she was of her husband.

Our next blessing of the year was getting to hold our new grandson when we got home from the trip to Spokane. Our son, his wife, daughter and new baby would be in our area for a month as they transferred to a new Marine Corp unit in California. I even got to watch the baby overnight, which made me a bit nervous as I had not had to do that in ten years. I warned the girls at the church that I may be late for Sunday school and asked them to cover for me till I got down there. To my surprise, I walked into church, baby in arms, with 15 minutes to spare. I just smiled at the girls and said with a wink, "I still got it. This ain't my first rodeo."

Later in the summer, I was blessed by being able to go back to Gillette, Wyoming with Christopher and Eli to help celebrate my mother's surprise 65th birthday party that my sisters-in-law and I had arranged. As if spending a week with my brothers and other family members was not a big enough blessing, God rained more upon me.

The first weekend I was there, I got together with my mother-in-law and spent the day with her. She spoiled me absolutely rotten. We went yard saling (something we had not done in years), she bought me several new outfits and took me out to lunch. My father-in-law, in the meantime, had called and asked if he could take Chris and Eli for the afternoon. Being so far away, they had not gotten the opportunity to spend much time with their Grandpa. He spent time with them and took them to lunch. I knew this was a direct result from prayer. We had been praying for his parents every night since we started praying together and I could see how God was helping us to draw nearer to each other. I felt it was a new start to a relationship with my in-laws that I was excited to nourish.

My next blessing was having the opportunity to write some articles for a new book that was coming out. I had met the publisher through a Bible study that this woman had written. She was a very down-to-earth gal and the timing in which we met was very God orchestrated. Her study entitled The Fine Art of Female Friendship was handed to me the very week I was struggling with being lonely. I asked the woman who gave it to me "Are you kidding me? Out of all the subjects in all the world and all the weeks of all the year, why this one now?"

As I began the study on my own , I went through a whole gamete of emotions. I saw that the author had put her email address on the back of the book. I felt compelled to write to her and tell her how God had used her in my life. I decided to teach this study to the women of the church and the author agreed to come and help me kick it off. I was thrilled! A real author and publisher would be in my midst and I was very intimidated.

She kept in close contact with me as she inquired about the class and then sent an email inviting women to write about relationships. I have always had a desire to write and wrote a lot during high school. I had put my pen down for many years and it was not until about two years before this that I had picked it back up again to write some poetry. I decided to dig through what I had and came up with two poems and then wrote an essay about the impact that women have on the lives of those around them. All three items were accepted for her book and I was on cloud nine.

I did have to giggle when I looked at the date that the book was due to come out. It was September 15. September has always been a very hard month for me to get through. It SEEMED as though anything bad that happened to me always happened in September. Annually, I struggled mentally, emotionally and spiritually through that month. I was determined to not let September get the best of me this year. Remember, I was choosing to have a wonderful year and was not going to let this one month ruin it for me. I was going to finally grab on to the healing that God had wanted me to have for so long. To reward me for my efforts, He had this book come out in September. He was trying to turn that month around for me. I love the things our Father does for us. He is so amazing!

Learning the business side of writing through workshops that I attended with this same author/ publisher is what spurred me on to this project. Dallas and I had talked many times about writing information down that we could share with other churches and sell in book form. I was thrilled to have the opportunity to "learn the ropes" ahead of time. I was ecstatic to be able to have the chance to figure out who I was going to be after the kids were gone and we were out of this part of ministering. My writing was something that was all mine.

As the year was coming to a close I noticed the opportunity was given to Dallas and I to witness to our adult children on a more regular basis. Our older children were still at home when we were just learning to seek a relationship with God ourselves. We had some warped thoughts of what being a Christian consisted of. Dallas admitted he thought that the kids' relationship with God should look exactly like his. I thought that as long as my children were singing during worship service that we would be considered holy, along with many other legalistic behaviors. We have had to ask forgiveness from God and our children regarding our strict ways in that area because now we know how holy we are by how much of the Bible we have highlighted. I'm kidding! I just think that is funny.

Joyce Myers was teaching one day. She explained that many of us underline, highlight and star things in the Bible as we read. Then when we open up to one of those pages on Sunday morning we are just HOPING that somebody will see that page and notice how holy we are. We have made that our running joke in our leadership class.

My heart ached for my older children and I realized that it seemed much harder being a mother of an adult than those that were at home because of the lack of control I had. I didn't always know where the boundaries were. The one thing our kids were great at though was letting us speak freely about God. When the kids asked for advice, my husband was able to ask them if they wanted that advice from the perspective of a dad, a friend or a pastor. I really admired him for his discernment with that, because Dallas knew that if they wanted a friend to talk to, it meant they wanted someone that they were sure would back them up and be on their side. If they wanted it from Dad, they could expect things to be a little more logical in terms of guidance. If they truly wanted it from a pastor, they knew Dallas had no problem telling them exactly what the Word had to say about the topic at hand. That aspect actually worked its way into the dad and friend advice also.

We prayed every night for our daughter, Desire and son, Jordan, that God would protect their hearts, minds and spirits. For our oldest son, David, we prayed for him to see the importance of taking his wife and children to church. He was a great dad and a doting husband. He knew church was the right thing to do.

It would break my heart as I would watch our 22 year old daughter, Patricia and 21 year old son, JJ try to figure out the responsibility of adulthood. Reality hit them hard and it was not easy. The fun part though was watching them seek for answers.

I tried to encourage them that God was going to reward them for digging for the truth. Patricia mostly just needed the encouragement to keep on doing her best. JJ was the one we would have deep philosophical conversations with. He would come to our church on Sundays and began attending our leadership class as we were going through the Doctrine study that was really dissecting who God was.

We loved being able to direct our kids in this way. One of my favorite sayings is "They are defenseless against our prayers!" I have seen this on so many levels in relationships. Some work in relationships and situations can only be done through prayer.

It amazed me the blessings that were pouring into my life when I was willing to open my eyes and ask God to cleanse my heart. I kept a journal of my prayers and when those prayers were answered. It was a great encouragement for me to go to that journal in times of trial to remind myself just how faithful our Almighty God is.

Occurrence:
Wanting blessings
Solution:
Obey and Pray

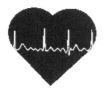

12
ALTARS OF STONE

Henry Blackaby's study, Experiencing God, gave a great illustration with a road marked periodically with a pile of rocks representing an altar. He explained that "often men in the Old Testament set up a stone marker or altar as a reminder of their encounters with God" and they provided an opportunity for people to teach their children about the activity of God. If you think about what God has done in your life, you can see certain dates or times that made an impact on you or took you to a different level. Those are places that you could have built an altar and given a name to God portraying how He helped in that time of your life.

I challenge you to write down some times in your journey that you could have placed an altar to see the order God has placed in your life through the sequence of these stepping stones. Blackaby explains that "every act of God builds on the past with a view toward the future." We need to remember our God is a God of order, right from the very beginning with the order in which He created things each day on down to the details in each of our lives. He is a God of order and we need to praise Him for that!

After you write down your altar moments, think about what name you would have given God at those times in your life. Moses named one of his altars, The Lord is my Banner. Samuel named a stone Ebenezer saying , "Thus far has the Lord helped us." What names does God have in your life? Was He your Shelter From the Storm (**Isaiah 25:4**), your Avenger (**Psalm 18:47**), your Peace (**I Thessalonions 5:23**), your Comforter (**II Corinthians 1:3**), your Protector? Was He your Revealer of Truth? This activity will open your eyes to see how God has had His hand on you from the very beginning.

I have learned a lot in the short journey I have had so far as a pastor's wife and I am glad to report that I am looking forward to being in the ministry, in some form or another, for the rest of my life. I know there is much more I need to learn, but I'm willing to be taught now. There is so much work to be done for the Kingdom of God that there should never be a dull moment.

I know now what happens behind the scenes of ministry. I will never take for granted the people that work in ministry, especially the women. It has made me more aware of the appreciation and encouragement I need to give to the wives involved. I pray that my illustrations and tips can be helpful to each reader.

A quick overview:

- Remember that God has a purpose for your life

- Remember Who you belong to – be confident in who He has created you to be. Your role is important (Proverbs 31).

- Be prepared in season and out.

- Do not let your past define you, let God mold you.

- Remember whose helpmeet you are – serve and protect.

- Communicate.

- Know when to pick the mat up and when to put the mat down so as not to let bitterness set in.

- Setting boundaries is okay.

- Have your go to people.

- Consent to heart surgery when needed.

- Remember Who you are doing this for.

Occurrence:
Acknowledging God

Solution:
Set up an altar to remember. Give God a name for that situation.

ABOUT THE AUTHOR

JoEllen Claypool is a contributing author of An Eclectic Collage Volume 2: Relationships of Life. She is the wife of a Southern Baptist preacher and supports his vision to prepare the individual members of the church body to become Kingdom builders. JoEllen and her husband, Dallas, share the joys of being homeschooling parents, teaching the two youngest of seven children. They are working toward the goal of writing books together and speaking encouragement to other churches.

ENDNOTES

Michael. DVD. Directed by Nora Ephron. 1996; Burbank, CA: Warner Home Video, 1997.

Decluttering, www.flylady.net visited 09/2010

Freund, Jane. <u>The Fine Art of Female Friendship</u>, Boise, ID: Freundship Press, 2012

eHow Health Article on Heart Disease. 1999-2012. Demand Media, Inc., visited 08/2011

"Enjoying Everyday Life." Joyce Meyer Ministries, The Word Network. Television

Blackaby, Henry. <u>Experiencing God</u>, Nashville, TN, B & H Publishing Group, 1998

Terkeurst, Lysa. <u>What Happens When Women Walk in Faith</u>, Eugene, OR: Harvest House Publishers, 2005